My shelves are full of books abou[t]
but Pauline's new book is outsta[nding]
thoughtful, grounded in personal [...]
fruit of a lifetime of international ministry and friendship,
and deep engagement with God's Word. To those
beginning with the Bible, Pauline passes on a wealth of
practical insights, and more seasoned readers will be
challenged to think more widely and more wisely.

Jenny Petersen

Chaplain at Queen Mary College, University of London

In this excellent book about Bible engagement, Pauline
Hoggarth shows at the same time the depth and width of
her acquaintance with the Bible, and her rich experience
of many years working around the world encouraging
people to get into the Book. Her global experience and
her teaching ability, take us to cross the missionary
frontiers of the twenty-first century with a renewed
confidence in the life giving and transforming
power of Scripture.

Samuel Escobar

Professor Emeritus of Missiology, Palmer Theological Seminary

Reading Pauline Hoggarth's book, one is aware that
everything she writes is deeply rooted in her own life of
engagement with Scripture and in her wide experience
of the Bible's impact in many different cultural contexts.
She is refreshingly open about both the difficulties
many people have in engaging with Scripture and the
difficulties Scripture itself presents. In addition, it is a
pleasure to read a book about engagement with the
Bible that is itself engagingly written.

Richard Bauckham

Emeritus Professor of New Testament Studies, University of St. Andrews

The Seed and the Soil

 Global Christian Library

Titles in this series:

The Seed and the Soil

Engaging with the Word of God

Pauline Hoggarth

Series Editor: David Smith
Consulting Editor: Joe Kapolyo

 **Global Christian Library**

Published 2011 by Global Christian Library
an imprint of Langham Creative Projects

Langham Partnership International
PO Box 296, Carlisle, Cumbria, CA3 9WZ

www.langhampartnership.org

First published 2011

British Library Cataloguing-in-Publication Data

A catalogue record of this book is available from the British Library.

ISBN: 978-1-907713-09-5

Cover design: projectluz.com

Book design: To a Tee Ltd, www.2at.com

CONTENTS

To Kit and Angie Inchley, for friendship

SERIES PREFACE

This book forms part of the Global Christian Library series published by Langham Literature, a subdivision of Langham Partnership International.

The twentieth century saw a dramatic shift in the Christian centre of gravity. There are now many more Christians in Africa, Asia and Latin America than there are in Europe and North America. Two major issues have resulted, both of which the Global Christian Library seeks to address.

First, the basic theological texts available to pastors, students and lay readers in the Majority World (sometimes referred to as the Developing World) have for too long been written by Western authors from a Western perspective. There is now a need for more books by non-Western writers that reflect their own cultures. In consequence, the Global Christian Library includes work by gifted writers from the developing world who are resolved to be biblically faithful and contextually relevant.

Second, Western readers need to be able to benefit from the wisdom and insight of our sisters and brothers in other parts of the world. Given the decay of many Western churches, we urgently need an injection of non-Western Christian vitality

The adjective 'global' in the title of this series reflects our desire that biblical understanding will flow freely in all directions. We pray that the Global Christian Library will open up channels of communication, in fulfilment of the Apostle Paul's conviction that it is only together with all the Lord's people that we will be able to grasp the dimensions of Christ's love (Eph 3:18).

Never before in the church's long history has this possibility been so close to realization. We hope and pray that the Global Christian Library may play a part in making it a reality in the twenty-first century.

Joe M. Kapolyo
David W. Smith

PREFACE

Some time in the early 1980s, exploring the shelves of the San Pablo bookshop in La Paz, Bolivia, I came across a shabby, mimeographed booklet with an intriguing title. *Biblia: Flor Sin Defensa (The Bible: Defenseless Flower)* described the experiences of a Dutch Carmelite priest working in Brazil and witnessing what happened when marginalized and poor communities and individuals began to engage with the Bible. As I leafed through the booklet, trying to decide if it was worth buying, one sentence leapt off the page: 'The Bible either helps or hinders, either liberates or oppresses. It is not neutral.'

The book you're now reading seems to me to be rooted in my discovery of that unimpressive booklet and in the years that followed of reflection on that statement. I owe a great debt of gratitude to Carlos Mesters for helping me both to understand my own imprisoning and liberating experiences of the Bible, and to explore the kind of Bible engagement that sets people free to know and live the truth of God.

It was while I was still working in Bolivia that a friend lent me a book by another author who has been formative in my thinking about Scripture and to whom I want to say a very warm thank you. Eugene Peterson's reflections on the book of Jeremiah, *Run with the Horses*, refreshed and energized me at a time when the Bible had become a dry textbook. Ever since, I have found Peterson's writing unfailingly refreshing, unfailingly building my confidence in God's word.

My warmest thanks go also to the worldwide Scripture Union fellowship with which I've had the privilege and enjoyment of working for some twenty-three years. These years are reflected on pretty well every page of this book! Thank you to Colin Matthews for leading a Bible Ministries Department in London back in the 1990s that was characterized by humour and lively theological debate. Thank you to Danilo Gay and John Lane for their friendship, encouragement and for asking stretching questions about our ways of working with the Bible.

Every workshop - from Sarawak to Guatemala, Latvia to Armenia - has been a rich learning experience for me, as we have explored together how God's word addresses each different context.

Thank you too to friends and colleagues in the Forum of Bible Agencies International and particularly the Scripture Engagement Group. What a privilege – and how much fun! - it has been to work together as different Bible agencies on exploring interaction with the Bible and experiencing God's word doing its work among us, changing us and our perspectives.

My colleagues on the small international Scripture Union team have also made major contributions to this book. The chapter titled 'Young Word' reflects so much that I have learned from travelling and working together with Wendy Strachan, our children's ministry coordinator. Clayton Fergie has been a great encourager through his gift for taking ideas that I have shared with him and developing them into workshop resources. My warmest thanks go to Wendy and Clay and to Janet Morgan who, as SU's international director, has been so encouraging about this project and generous in giving me time to write.

One small group of people has been especially significant in helping me to complete this book. Jock Stein, Sybil Davis, Ruth Pinkerton and Elizabeth McDowell have been members of an accountability group with whom I've met regularly for the last ten years. They have encouraged and urged me on over the embarrassingly long time it has taken to complete the work. Jock's experience of writing and publishing has been especially helpful. In the last months of writing, Jenny Hyatt's editorial experience was invaluable in shaping the manuscript. I couldn't have done it without her help. Thank you so much to you all.

I want to say thank you also to Angelit Guzmán in Peru, Bob Ekblad in Seattle, David Zac Niringiye in Uganda, David Bruce in Northern Ireland, Daniel Besse and Henri Bacher in France and Silvia Regina de Lima Silva in Costa Rica for all they have taught me about life-giving and creative Scripture engagement. For reading various chapters and making helpful suggestions and comments, I'm indebted to Jenny Petersen, Allen Goddard, Joyce Smith, Chris Wright and Leanne Palmer.

Dr David Smith was the managing editor at the time when I joined this writing project. Without his kindly encouragement and patient and perceptive guidance, this book would never have been finished. Thank you so much, David, not just for your help with this book, but for your own books which have enriched my thinking and deepened my trust in God and his word.

Pauline Hoggarth
Strathkinness, Fife, December 2010

1

Transforming Word

Indeed, the word of God is living and active
— **Hebrews 4:12**

'What's wrong with my heart? My heart is hurting. What's wrong?' Among Quechua-speaking communities in Bolivia, this has been the consistent response of men and women as they listen together to chapter 5 of Mark's Gospel recorded in their mother tongue.[1] They cry out as they hear Jesus ask, 'Who touched my clothes?' (Mark 5:30). They weep at his tender welcome of the outcast woman: 'Daughter, your faith has made you well; go in peace, and be healed of your disease' (Mark 5:34). In this Bible story above all others, these despised people rediscover themselves as they meet Jesus. Since the Spanish Conquest in the sixteenth century, their oppressors have dismissed the Quechua as worthless, primitive and unclean. Now they hear Jesus' welcome, see him pause and stand still, his attention focused fully on a woman who in significant ways shares their experience of exclusion. The living word of Scripture touches – even 'hurts' – their hearts and opens the way for them to have courage also to reach out to Jesus and trust his welcome.

Some two thousand years earlier, on the desert road between Jerusalem and Gaza, a man who was in many ways excluded like the Quechua also encountered Scripture's power to prompt urgent questions (Acts 8:26–39). Reading aloud to himself from the scroll of Isaiah, a senior civil servant at the Ethiopian court who was also a eunuch[2] suddenly found a man called Philip running alongside his chariot. Mysteriously impelled to this encounter by God's Holy Spirit, Philip had been listening to the man reading and was concerned to know if he needed help to understand. 'Yes, I do. Who is the prophet talking about?' The conversation that followed moved outwards,

Luke tells us, from Isaiah's vision to all 'the good news about Jesus'. Philip was able to help this man discover how in Jesus the prophet's revelations were fulfilled, especially in their depiction of the 'God of the whole earth' (Isa. 54:5), who lovingly and generously summons all the nations (Isa. 55:3–5) and welcomes anxious foreigners and despised eunuchs (Isa. 56:3–8). Like the Bolivian Quechua, this man 'went on his way rejoicing', the first African to come to faith in Jesus and identify with him in baptism.

Not far from the eunuch's home country, and many centuries later, a woman called Nurat encountered the power of God's word to cut to the heart of human experience and bring about transformation. She was a Muslim, listening to Scripture broadcast over the sound system of the local church. The thin bamboo walls allowed the recordings to be heard in most of the village. Nurat already knew about Jesus from the Qur'an's account of him as God's messenger. Now she kept hearing about Jesus' miracles and healings and wondered how she might truly find him. In her heart she felt the urge to bring one problem to him to see what he would do. Her marriage was a constant struggle. She would become angry with her husband and refuse to talk to him. He behaved violently towards her and insulted her family and friends. Eventually she decided to bring the problem of her marriage to the Lord. Soon after this, listening again to the audio Scriptures, she heard words from one of Paul's letters that touched her deeply. They described many of the things that characterized her life: 'Now the works of the flesh are obvious ... idolatry, sorcery ... strife ... anger, quarrels ... those who do such things will not inherit the kingdom of God' (Gal. 5:19–21). Responding to Paul's words as if they were addressed to her personally, Nurat stopped going to consult her father who was a sorcerer and did her best to be less angry towards her husband. He began to notice the change in her, started to listen himself to the Bible recordings, and eventually became a follower of Jesus alongside his wife.

Engaging with God's word as a call to action can be painful and demand courageous choices. In an East Asian country whose powerful elites are notorious for breaking the laws that protect the forests and those who live in them, a Christian doctor has chosen to leave the calm waters of his successful medical practice and sail out into the stormy seas of politics. He says: 'I read in Scripture of the sovereign rule of God in this world, of his love of justice and his concern for powerless people. Behind the Bible text I see the faces of villagers I know who have lost their land to logging companies. If these people are to put their trust in God, then his sovereignty and love of justice have to be more than a matter of words on a page for them; they must become reality in their lives. This is why I entered politics.'[3] Many of his fellow-Christians do not share this man's understanding of Scripture's call to action. They believe that politics is a murky business in which Christians should not be involved. There has been, at least initially, little encouragement or prayer support for his response to God's word.

From Europe comes evidence of the power of Scripture to change an entire worldview. This is David's story:

> I am a Protestant from Northern Ireland. My unhappiness at describing myself in such terms today is because of the impact of two things: the murder of my friend, and the Bible. I became a Christian in 1975 when the 'Troubles' were at their height. In Northern Ireland the 'Troubles' means the civil conflict that raged since the formation in 1922 of Northern Ireland as a compromise political solution to the wider Irish problem that had been rumbling on for centuries. My childhood was a privileged, middle-class, Protestant experience in which I was largely protected from the harsh realities of life on the streets of Belfast or Derry. At boarding school I grew up in my sheltered circle to believe not very much about anything. In Northern Ireland terms I was a 'passive bigot'. I had no Catholic friends; I lived, socialised, learned and played in an entirely Protestant environment. School led seamlessly to university in Belfast where at the age of eighteen I came to faith in Christ – and became an active bigot. Through teaching received in those first years of my Christian life I came to believe that the Pope was the antichrist and that Roman Catholicism was a Satan-inspired plot to undermine the true faith of the Bible. I became completely unable to relate normally to Catholic people, even on a superficial level. I tried to justify this disturbing problem (and I did find it disturbing) by saying that I loved individual Catholics but couldn't accept Roman Catholicism as a system. In truth I was a bigot who did not want to relate to anyone outside my tribe.
>
> John Donaldson was one of my circle at school. We did our undergraduate studies together, he in law and I in social studies. Through the Christian Union, we became close friends. We graduated on the same day and John began to work with a law firm in Belfast, while I went to Scotland to start my studies in theology. When I heard on 12 October 1979 that there had been another shooting in Belfast, I hardly gave it a thought. Killings in Belfast were commonplace. But

something caught my attention in a later news bulletin and I phoned home to discover that John had been shot dead while delivering legal papers to a police station in west Belfast. One of the Irish Republican terrorist factions had mistaken him for an undercover agent for the British security forces.

I was devastated and outraged by John's death. I wanted God to consume his killers with fire and I explained what had happened by adding another strand to the partnership of evil already established in my mind. Not only was Roman Catholicism a Satan-inspired plot, so was Irish Republicanism. Like many of my fellow citizens, I came to believe that the aims of the Roman Catholic Church and the violent terrorist organisations made up of its members were the same – to destroy the Protestant, unionist people of Northern Ireland. The task of Christian mission was therefore to resist Irish republicanism and Roman Catholicism by all and every means.

At the time of my friend's murder I was studying theology in preparation for ordination in the Presbyterian Church. Christ's College, Aberdeen seemed a world away from Belfast. Among others, Professor James Torrance offered me deep understanding and pastoral compassion as I worked through the impossibility of loving John's killers. 'Christ died for them, David,' was his repeated response in my anguish. I began to read the New Testament again, as I had never read it before. If Christ died for John's killers, then he must indeed have loved them – much as he loved Samaritans and Romans in his own day. And if he loved them, then so must I. Furthermore, if Jesus-the-Jew loved Gentiles, then I had no basis for excluding a person from the scope of God's grace on the basis of ethnic origin or political beliefs – something Paul demonstrated with extraordinary courage by going to share Jesus with the Gentiles he had been nurtured to despise. Acts 22 changed my life. Piece by piece, over a period of two years, my theology of bigotry was dismantled. I have come to see that the Bible is a handbook of anti-sectarianism, a narrative that will not permit us to believe in a God who is other than the God of all peoples.

A Protestant from Northern Ireland? Today I would rather be described as a follower of Jesus living in Ireland, because I want the door to my home and my heart to be open to a relationship with the people who killed my friend.[4]

David's rediscovery and new understanding of familiar Scripture in the midst of personal crisis has many parallels in the account in Luke 24 of the meeting on the Emmaus road between the risen Jesus and Cleopas and his companion. Like David, these disciples were familiar with Scripture and read it with the certainties and prejudices of their national context. In David's case his understandings, shaped by his social and theological milieu, provided justification for bigotry and sectarianism. In the case of the two on the Emmaus road, their understanding of Scripture added up to a political Messiah 'mighty in deed and word before God and all the people' who would liberate their nation (Luke 24:19, 21). The death of David's friend John left him utterly disarmed, able only to pray for a fiery end for the killers. The execution on a Roman cross of Jesus, friend of these two disciples, left them bereft and despairing. David's patient and compassionate teacher helped him to re-examine his rage and grief; his perspective ('Christ died for them, David') provoked his student to a radically new reading and understanding of the Bible. On the Emmaus road, Jesus himself walked with the disciples and unfolded to them an entirely different way of hearing the evidence of Scripture about himself, one that turned them round in their tracks: 'Were not our hearts burning within us … while he was opening the scriptures to us?' (Luke 24:32).

News of the impact of Scripture sometimes reaches us – perhaps most surprisingly and encouragingly – through the secular media. In an *Observer* article in October 1999, political commentator Will Hutton wrote,

> So who said religion was dead and there was no God? … The Jubilee 2000 campaign has proved to be one of the most effective ever mounted by any pressure group; it may secure an end that four years ago seemed a pipedream – the cancellation of the unpayable debt owed by the world's poorest countries.
>
> But it owes its success and inspiration to the Bible. I doubt many readers know the Old Testament books of Leviticus, Exodus and Deuteronomy any more than I do, but without them there would be no Jubilee 2000, no debt campaign and no international public pressure. At the end of an increasingly secular century, it has been the biblical proof and moral imagination of religion that have torched the principles of the hitherto unassailable citadels of international finance – and opened the way to a radicalism about capitalism whose ramifications are not yet fully understood.

Just glance at the blessing the Pope gave to the Jubilee campaigners before the IMF / World Bank meetings this year. The Catholic Church, he said, has always taught there was a 'social mortgage' on all private property. 'The law of profit alone cannot be applied to that which is essential for the fight against hunger, disease and poverty.' ... The Pope, like the Church of England, is simply following the injunction of the Bible, and in particular Leviticus Chapter 25, a passage that makes Das Kapital look tame. Leviticus tells its readers that God designed the world to be in harmony, and that every seven years creditors should offer debtors a remission – or repayment holiday. But every seven times seven years ... there should be a Sabbath's Sabbath; a complete dismantling of the structures of social and economic inequality. Debts should be forgiven completely, slaves freed and land forfeited for non-payment of debt returned to its original owners, a principle endorsed both by Exodus and Deuteronomy. The Bible is unambiguous ... The Left of Centre should take note; it is no longer Morris, Keynes and Beveridge who inspire and change the world – it's Leviticus.[5]

Andrew Rugasira, a Christian businessman from Uganda, would endorse this understanding of the radical nature of the Bible and its power to bring about change. He features in a newspaper article that describes what he has done to enable coffee growers in the Rwenzori Mountains of northern Uganda to sell their produce directly to supermarkets in the UK and elsewhere. Rugasira's Good Africa Coffee Company shares profits with these farmers on a revolutionary 50:50 basis; the company's slogan is 'Trade not Aid'. The article tells an inspiring story of community transformation taking place among people who for years have been terrorized by the soldiers of Obote, Amin and most recently Congolese rebels. The journalist who wrote the article reports several times that he noticed Rugasira reading his Bible as he went about his work. Clearly the journalist had made some kind of connection between Rugasira's Bible reading and the activities in which he was involved.[6] I wanted to hear from Andrew Rugasira how he understood that connection, so I wrote to him via his company's website. He wrote back immediately:

My link between Bible engagement and community transformation is in the value system of the Word. The more we engage and internalize the word of God, submit to its authority, truth and guidance, the more community transformation becomes a critical

element of our life's mission here on earth. But one has to make a
choice: take the Bible as a call to action or treat it as an ideal too
remote to be acted upon.[7]

Community transformation is at the heart of two Old Testament narratives
that describe the rediscovery of God's word by his people, and its impact on
them. Six centuries before Christ, Josiah was a reforming king in Judah. At
the age of sixteen, despite being son and grandson of Amon and Manasseh,
two of Judah's most corrupt rulers, Josiah 'began to seek the God of his
ancestor David' (2 Chr. 34:3). Four years later, perhaps encouraged by the
prophet Jeremiah, he began to rid the land of everything to do with the
decadent Assyrian religious cults. But it was when he was twenty-six that
Josiah's reforms took on new energy. The impulse came through the discovery
in the temple by Hilkiah the high priest of 'the book of the law' (possibly a
version of the book of Deuteronomy). The king's secretary Shaphan reads the
scroll aloud to the king, whose response is immediate and dramatic. He rips
his clothes in consternation, 'for great is the wrath of the Lord that is kindled
against us, because our ancestors did not obey the words of this book, to do
according to all that is written concerning us' (2 Kgs 22:13). The prophetess
Huldah confirms that Josiah is right in his response to God's rediscovered
word: his people do indeed stand under God's judgment (2 Kgs. 22:14–20).
There follows the account of Josiah's root and branch reforms that start with
the public reading of Scripture:

> The king went up to the house of the Lord, and with him went all the
> people … both small and great; he read in their hearing all the words
> of the book of the covenant that had been found in the house of the
> Lord. The king stood by the pillar and made a covenant before the
> Lord, to follow the Lord … to perform the words of this covenant
> that were written in this book. All the people joined in the covenant
> (2 Kgs. 23:2, 3).

But with few exceptions the people of Judah did not, in Andrew Rugasira's
words, 'engage and internalize the word of God' other than superficially and
sporadically. So God allowed the Babylonian empire to be the instrument
of judgment on Judah's failure to demonstrate to the peoples around them
the beauty, integrity and justice of his ways. Some two centuries after Josiah
we find some of them living under Persian rule in a burned out and ruined
Jerusalem, their only hope two leaders – Nehemiah and Ezra – who do

indeed submit to the authority, truth and guidance of the word of God. Ezra is described as someone who 'had set his heart to study the law of the Lord, and to do it, and to teach the statutes and ordinances in Israel' (Ezra 7:10). Most remarkably, the Persian king Artaxerxes came to respect this scholar and doer of God's word, and allowed him to return to Jerusalem with those of his people who wanted to go with him (Ezra 7:12–28). Similarly, the book of Nehemiah records how profoundly this leader prayed and lived out God's word, identifying with his people's sin, recognizing the justice of God's judgment and pleading for his mercy (Neh. 1:8–9). The book of Nehemiah tells of the impact of the public reading of God's word on the community:

> So they read from the book, from the law of God, with interpretation.
> They gave the sense, so that the people understood the reading. And
> ... all the people wept when they heard the words of the law ... And
> all the people went their way ... to make great rejoicing, because
> they had understood the words that were declared to them (Neh.
> 8:8–12).

The community in Jerusalem responded with their minds and with their hearts – intellectually and emotionally – to the word of God that they heard.

One final testimony in this chapter to the power of God's word also speaks of this double response. Miltos Anghelatos came from a Greek Orthodox family in Corfu. At the age of twenty, he was in despair. 'Intellectually, I stumbled in darkness and confusion. Morally, I wallowed in passion and lies and sin. Mentally I was wavering and in despair.'[8] One day, reading Dostoyevsky's novel *The Brothers Karamazov* he noticed words on the title page that puzzled him: 'Verily, verily, I say unto you, except a corn of wheat fall into the ground and die, it abideth alone: but if it die, it bringeth forth much fruit' (John 12:24). The words intrigued Miltos but he had no idea who John was, or what the numbers referred to. His English teacher explained that they came from the Bible. Miltos asked what the Bible was. His teacher told him it was a book that people called missionaries had taken to the South Sea Islands. When they had given this book to the cannibals, the cannibals stopped eating people. This information made Miltos determined to get hold of a Bible. He finally found a second-hand one in Corfu and bought it in exchange for eight pounds of potatoes – a high price in 1942. 'The next day, sitting on the small hill behind our house, I sat with the Holy Book of God open in my hands.' Over the next months, Miltos read the Bible for over ten hours a day:

> Nothing could withstand the light of this book of God … In no way
> could I excuse myself … At last I came to the end of my tether. That
> afternoon, like the magicians of old, I brought out the archives of
> the life I had led before I knew Christ, my books, my pictures, my
> writings, and threw them all on to the fire. Then I knelt down. I
> did not say much. It was tears that gave me tongue. In shame and
> repentance I brought to the foot of the cross of Christ the whole of
> my liabilities, all my sins which the Holy Spirit had brought to my
> memory. I felt in the very depths of my soul the joyful assurance
> that 'the blood of Jesus Christ cleanseth you from all your sin'. In
> my diary I wrote, 'I stop keeping this diary, because I am entering,
> or rather I have been reborn, into a new life. I have discovered the
> truth I was searching for. I did not find it in human wisdom but in
> the Gospel of my Lord Jesus Christ.'[9]

Miltos's father was furious at what had happened. 'The Bible will make you bankrupt,' he shouted, and threw the dog-eared book on the fire. Thrown out of his home, Miltos left Corfu and went to Athens where a Christian pastor and his wife took him in. He worked as a civil servant, but in his spare time he welcomed children to the meetings he organized for them, and started a small publishing programme. The work of Scripture Union in Greece today traces its beginnings to Miltos Anghelatos's transforming encounter with God's word.

The common thread running through all these stories is the interaction or engagement of an individual or a community with Scripture, either heard or read. This interaction has profound consequences for life, transforming understandings, attitudes and worldviews, impelling people in new directions, drawing them into a new relationship with God. The despised Quechua suddenly understand their dignity as human beings, their identity as recipients of God's love and acceptance; the Ethiopian courtier becomes a follower of Jesus; Nurat is convicted of her need to change and develop new attitudes to her husband and father. A doctor's life takes a dramatic and demanding new direction; David rejects his sectarian culture and opens his heart to people he regarded as the 'enemy'; the Emmaus couple race back to Jerusalem to communicate a transformed understanding of Jesus' – and their own – identity and purpose. A journalist acknowledges the power of an ancient text to 'torch the principles of the hitherto unassailable citadels of international finance'[10]; Andrew Rugasira pioneers a new model of trade agreement to benefit exploited communities; Josiah, Ezra and Nehemiah take brave reforming decisions, and their people – at least for a time – follow their lead because the word of God has engaged their minds and hearts. And Miltos Anghelatos finally discovers the truth he has been searching for – and becomes an outcast from his family. These people have all encountered and responded to a word that claims to be 'able to judge the thoughts and intentions of the heart' (Heb. 4:12).

Alongside this unifying theme is the uniqueness of each encounter. God's word takes some of our witnesses by surprise – they hear it 'by accident' – while others desperately and intentionally search the Bible for answers to their anguish. For some, the encounter with Scripture is the start of a life of following Jesus; for others, listening to God in the Bible is already a habit of life that constantly keeps them on their toes as they respond to what they are discovering. In each case, the individual or community recognizes significant connections between what is happening in their lives and what they are hearing or reading in Scripture. But the words that impact on them are all different, ranging from Gospel narratives and Old Testament prophecy to Paul's letters, from precepts in Leviticus and Deuteronomy to the autobiography of Acts 22. The ancient words of Scripture constantly take on new life as they intersect with the unique current circumstances and needs of each person or community.

Before reading further, you might like to take time to think about your own story of how the Bible has made a mark on your life and/ or the life of your community. What have been the turning points, the changes and new understandings that have come about because you and/or your community interacted with the word of God? You could draw a simple 'route map' of your life and mark those turning points on it.

The stories in this chapter represent a minute sample of what is happening and has happened down the centuries as men, women, children and entire communities encounter God's word. The Internet, books and magazines give us access to many more witnesses to the impact of God's word across the world. Appendix 1, on page 143, lists some of these resources.

All these testimonies – those that are internal to Scripture and those we might call external evidence, coming from our contemporaries – invite us to explore the nature of the Bible. What is the source of its transforming power? Is Scripture *automatically* transformational or are there preconditions for it to have such impact in people's lives? The Lausanne Covenant has this to say about the Bible:

> We … affirm the power of God's word to accomplish his purpose of salvation. The message of the Bible is addressed to all men and women. For God's revelation in Christ and in Scripture is unchangeable. Through it the Holy Spirit still speaks today. He illumines the minds of God's people in every culture to perceive its truth freshly through their own eyes and thus discloses to the whole Church ever more of the many-coloured wisdom of God.[11]

But today in the so-called developed world, even among churches that would call themselves Bible-centred, Scripture is increasingly marginalized; there is a serious crisis of confidence in the Bible as a place of true encounter with God. Along with the scriptures of other faiths, it is often dismissed as a closed and oppressive narrative, to be viewed with suspicion. In many parts of the Majority World, where the Bible may still be regarded respectfully as authoritative, it is in practice often used as a talisman, kept under the pillow to ward off evil, or invoked and interpreted to support power-seeking agendas (as it is elsewhere in the world).

The rest of this book will seek to explore what the Bible is and how it 'works'. Chapter 2, for example, will look at how and why we may resist the word of God or distort it to serve our own ends. Throughout the book we will try to identify those factors that seem to be crucial if God's word is to bring about change in us, and what seem to be the obstacles to transformation. You might look back over the 'witness statements' in this chapter and identify some of the conditions that seem to create the most hopeful context for Scripture to take effect.

I want to close this chapter with some memorable words that we will take up later as we explore the nature of the Bible:

> From a Christian perspective, God is first and foremost a communicative agent, one who relates to humankind through words and the Word … God is a speaking God … Most of what God does – creating, warning, commanding, promising, forgiving, informing,

comforting, etc. – is accomplished by speech acts ... The triune God is ... the epitome of communicative agency: the speech agent who utters, embodies, and keeps his Word ... Readers who work and pray over the text ... and who follow its itineraries of meaning, will be progressively transformed into the image of him who is the ultimate object of the biblical witness ... These are the interpreter-believers who, like the psalmist, take up their book and walk: 'Your word is a lamp to my feet and a light for my path' (Ps. 119:105).[12]

2

Resisted Word

Now the serpent ... said to the woman, 'Did God say ...?'
— **Genesis 3:1**

'I know that God's word asks me to make changes in my life and I'm fearful that I can't obey'; 'The Bible often feels like a stone on top of me, crushing me'; 'I struggle to see the relevance of Scripture to my life'; 'I often feel I never want to open the Bible again – it's too hard'; 'I wrestle with the seeming harshness of so much of Scripture'; 'I've had too many legalistic experiences of the Bible'; 'I simply don't experience the Bible as a place where God speaks to me'; 'I come to the Bible with low expectations of ever finding anything worthwhile there.'

Over a period of some ten years I've invited workshop participants to describe both their positive and problematic experiences of engaging with the Bible. The comments above represent a small sample of their difficult experiences, recorded verbatim. They come from people of different cultures and stages of the journey with God who also describe their many encouraging and exhilarating experiences of interacting with God's word. But it is the experiences of honest struggle that often lead to the most fruitful work of developing resources for Bible reflection, or of becoming the kind of person who can enable others to explore and live out God's word.

The witness of Scripture, from Genesis to Revelation, tells of the varied responses to God from men, women and children whose creation in his image includes the capacity to communicate and respond to communication. The story describes a God who makes himself known to humankind in often unspecified ways that the Bible invites us to imagine or guess at: in dreams and visions; through his chosen spokesmen and women; in creation; through the written records of his acts and will; and supremely in the person of Jesus, the living Word. How then are we to understand the range of responses to Scripture that include not only inspiring testimony to a life-changing engagement with God's word but also the troubling comments that open this chapter?

These seem to provide a clear answer to the question we raised in chapter 1. Does reading or listening to the Bible *automatically* bring about transformation 'into the image of him who is the ultimate object of the biblical witness'[13]? These honestly unhappy responses tell us that interaction with the Bible, even – perhaps especially – among Christian believers, may provoke resistance, anxiety, anger and disappointment. I want to explore this reality within the framework of Jesus' story of the farmer sowing his seed (Matt. 13:1–9; Mark 4:1–9; Luke 8:4–8). The narrative makes clear that while the quality of the seed remains constant, the ground into which it falls varies (the beaten track, the rocky terrain, the ground infested with thorny weeds, and the fertile earth). It is the soil that provides the seed with more or less chance of growing into a harvest. When Jesus explains the story to his disciples (Matt. 13:18–23; Mark 4:13–20; Luke 8:11–15), he highlights the active involvement of 'the evil one', in *taking away* the word from people's hearts. He also describes the problem of *superficial* engagement with God's word that doesn't stand testing times, and the reality of a context in which the word must *compete* with the demanding problems and pleasures of life. Jesus tells his disciples and us that even in the case of the seed that falls into good earth, its yield varies greatly.

Reflecting on his many years of encouraging marginalized communities in Brazil in their interaction with the Bible, the Dutch-born priest and Carmelite missionary Carlos Mesters acknowledges both the unfailing quality of the seed of God's word and the variety of its impact:

> The Bible either helps or hinders, either liberates or oppresses. It is not neutral. It is like a double-edged knife: it always cuts, for better or worse … the biblical text alone, or study of the text, is not enough to ensure the Bible will act as a contributor to liberation. The text is the same for everyone. What is not the same is its effect, and the obvious conclusion one can reach from that is that factors external to the text have much to do with whether the Bible functions as a liberative force in the people's lives.[14]

So what more can we learn by exploring the parable of the sower about these 'factors external to the text'? How do they work to prevent or enable our hearing the liberating 'word of the kingdom' (Matt. 13:19) and becoming transformed into the image of Jesus?

'Some seeds fell on the path, and the birds came and ate them up'
(Matt. 13:4)

In all three versions of Jesus' explanation of this parable to his disciples, he helps them to understand that the evil one hovers like a hungry bird over the well-trodden track to snatch away the truth of the word before it can penetrate and be so deeply understood that it bears fruit. What might this look like in our world today?

In a thought-provoking account of how his reflection on God's word and his work with prisoners and poor migrant workers have interacted with one another, Bob Ekblad, director of the Tierra Nueva (New Earth) community near Seattle, suggests that this aspect of the evil one's activities is evident in the very first communications between God and the human beings he has created. He describes first how the inmates of Skagit County Jail with whom he holds regular Bible studies hear the opening chapters of the Bible as a familiar story that makes sense of their present condition:

> The first humans disobey God's command of their own free will, so they deserve God's punishments. Sins have consequences. God acts swiftly to punish wrongdoing. Criminals who get caught can thus expect to be swiftly punished ... Everyone must submit to the moral order to be saved ... Everyone agrees that they see God as a judge and sin as disobedience.[15]

In the Bible study that follows this initial probing of the men's understanding of the narrative in Genesis 2 and 3, the prison inmates have an opportunity to examine again details of the story that they have forgotten or never been aware of, or have perhaps been encouraged in their religious traditions to pass over as insignificant. Ekblad suggests that they have always been on the receiving end of a 'dominant theology' that deals mostly in God as judge. Slowly, with the help of probing questions that take the men back again and again to the narrative details in Genesis, they uncover a different story.

The Genesis account opens with God's declarations to the first man and woman of generous provision and freedom: 'God blessed them, and God said to them, "Be fruitful and multiply, and fill the earth ... See, I have given you every plant ... and every tree with seed in its fruit; you shall have them for food" (Gen. 1:28–29). In the second version of the creation story in Genesis 2, God communicates the same generosity and freedom, this time to the man alone. But now he adds the warning of a caring parent: 'You may freely eat of every tree of the garden; but of the tree of the knowledge of good and evil you shall not eat, for in the day that you eat of it you shall die' (Gen. 2:16–17). In the encounter that follows in Genesis 3 between the serpent and the woman, we discover, not the birds of Jesus' parable of the sower, but the serpent, doing the same work of 'taking away' some of God's words from the woman's memory. The serpent subtly suggests to her a *partial* version of what God has said to the man. The man has presumably communicated to his companion an accurate version of God's words, and actually appears to be at the woman's side as the serpent speaks to her (Gen. 3:6). The serpent's version omits all mention of God's generous provision, and exaggerates his one exception into a complete ban: 'Did God say, "You shall not eat from any tree in the garden"?' (Gen. 3:1). The woman first timidly corrects the serpent's exaggeration ('We may eat of the fruit of the trees in the garden'), but then herself exaggerates God's one limitation on freedom ('You shall not eat of the fruit of the tree that is in the middle of the garden, *nor shall you touch it*, or you shall die', Gen. 3:2–3, my italics). The serpent now seems to sense the woman's hesitations and goes in for the kill; he bluntly contradicts God's lovingly concerned warning and invites the woman to imagine a seductive alternative: 'You will not die; for God knows that when you eat of it your eyes will be opened, and you will be like God, knowing good and evil' (Gen. 3:4–5).

I wonder how you respond to this reading of these familiar texts. Does it make you uneasy? Is it really legitimate to hear the words of Genesis 2:17 not as a declaration of judgment[16] but as a concerned warning from a loving God, the Creator who intimately knows his creation? Paul Ricoeur alerts us to the fact that 'we no longer know what a *limit* that does not repress, but orients and guards freedom, could be like … We are acquainted only with the limit that constrains.'[17] The more I have reflected on this text and understood how the serpent manipulates God's word at the very start of the biblical story, the more it seems to me that this is exactly what Jesus is describing in his parable, as he warns his disciples about the activity of the evil one in preventing an authentic understanding of what God wants to communicate.

This kind of distortion, this partial and selective remembering of God's word is powerfully effective in destroying true communication between God and those he has created. Genesis 3 makes clear that it is *fear* that now marks the response of the man and woman to God. The loving Creator has become the fearsome judge and we find ourselves saying, 'I often feel I never want to open the Bible again – it's too hard.' Trust, harmony and intimacy have gone (Gen. 3:8–13). Ekblad contrasts a way of interpreting the Bible that is primarily 'information about how people are supposed to live so as to please God', that is, a *moralizing* reading of Scripture, with a way of engaging with the Bible that looks first and foremost at what it *actually tells us about God*.[18] This kind of engagement will take us back to explore the narrative details and their wider context, seeking to make sure that the serpent voice has not been 'snatching away' crucial evidence that could drastically change our understanding. It will also enable us to come to the word of God with hope, trusting the Lord's promise that, 'If you continue in my word, you are truly my disciples; and you will know the truth, and the truth will make you free' (John 8:31).

Over several years of seeking to help the writers of Scripture Union's Bible guides in different countries to reflect on Scripture and explore its relationship to the contexts of their readers, I have come to understand that many of us (including myself) often fail to read the Bible as good news, as truth that sets us free. We have little expectation of discovering anything fresh. As one workshop participant commented, we have 'low expectations' of God's word. We believe we already know what Scripture says, and we continue to write or teach or preach 'eternal truths for the angels' (as a colleague of mine used to say), propositions that are unrelated to today's specific realities, and rarely anything that could truly be called 'good *news*'. I remember the comment of a friend who suggested that we may read the Ten Commandments either as a threatening, suffocating list of prohibitions, or as a prescription for life and health from a wise and compassionate physician. Try reading them aloud to yourself (Exod. 20:2–17). The tone of voice you choose may reflect the kind of God you have come to know.

Before we move on to look at the second kind of terrain that Jesus describes in his parable, it's crucial to notice that it is the *well-trodden path* that gives the birds the best chance to snatch the seed away. Might Jesus be pointing here to the way that familiar, culturally orthodox and routine understandings of God's word can create a hard-packed surface that makes it difficult for the ever-fertile seed of God's word to penetrate? In Luke's story of the Emmaus road that we have already looked at in chapter 1 in relation to David Bruce's testimony, Jesus offered the two distraught disciples an alternative understanding of 'well-trodden' Scriptures that utterly transformed their worldview (Luke 24:25–27). In his searching reflections on Luke's narrative, David Smith points out that Jesus' response to the disciples

> suggests that they are, at least in part, culpable in relation to their despair and hopelessness. Their desperation stems ultimately from their acceptance of a fundamentally mistaken worldview which was *based on a particular, and highly selective*, reading of the Hebrew Scriptures … they had … been misled by an ideological reading of the Bible … Now, as then, it is often the case, as Krister Stendahl observes, that our vision is more likely to be obstructed 'by what we think we know than by our lack of knowledge' … There is a question here for the modern church: if the prophetic texts of ancient Israel, originally so powerful and controversial … could, over the centuries, become neutered, read and heard within systems of interpretation that rendered them incapable   of disturbing the status quo or bringing about social and cultural transformation, might the same thing happen to the literature we know as the New Testament?[19]

What Jesus is doing on the Emmaus road is pointing to the 'dominant theology' of his age, another well-trodden, selective, doctrinal path that, until he opens up 'all the scriptures' (Luke 24:27), has made even his closest followers oblivious to the authentic good news of the kingdom of God.

Prejudiced, 'well-trodden' readings of Scripture can cause immense pain (the kind of pain we see in some of the comments at the start of this chapter). They can even be the cause of people giving up on the church and the Christian faith. A Nigerian friend, Olaniyi Daramola, told me the story of his birth in Ilesha. His mother struggled at home in labour for four long days while the elders of her church urged her to confess her sins so that God would forgive her and release the child. Finally her brother-in-law arrived and swiftly removed her to the hospital for a safe delivery. The elders were acting on the basis of a widely accepted legalistic and judgmental understanding of the Genesis story and especially a 'dominant theology' interpretation of Genesis 3:16.

I had a somewhat similar experience in the church of which I was a member in Bolivia. The congregation had proposed people to become elders and my name was put forward. The group of men in leadership took me aside and informed me that such a thing was impossible. Women had been responsible for all the heresies in the history of the church and the biblical case against women in church leadership was proven. They read me a range of Bible passages that, even at a time when I had not yet had cause to examine the evidence, struck me as being prejudiced and selective! It took a long time for things to heal, both in myself and between myself and the church leaders.

'Other seed fell on rocky ground, where it did not have much soil'
(Mark 4:5)

There are only slight differences in how the synoptic writers describe what happens to the seed that falls on rocky ground (Matt. 13:5–6; Mark 4:5–6; Luke 8:6). Matthew and Mark emphasize the shallow soil in which the seeds germinate fast. Unable to form proper roots, the new seedlings quickly shrivel under the blazing sun. Luke focuses on the inability of rock to hold moisture, so that the baby plants die. All three writers tell how Jesus draws the parallels between the first encouraging spurt of growth and the initial receptiveness ('joy') with which some people receive the news about God's kingdom, and then between the rapid withering of the seedlings under the sun and the falling away or 'stumbling' of these same people when they find themselves under pressure or in trouble. Matthew adds the detail of persecution that 'arises on account of the word' (Matt. 13:21).

Commenting on Revelation 10:8–11 Claudio Ettl of the Catholic Biblical Federation writes:

> God's word is not something we can stand looking at from a safe distance; rather, we can (and must) take it in our hands; it touches us in our innermost being. God's word wants to be swallowed and received in every conceivable sense. But at the same time it is no easily digestible fare, no prepared food; it must be well chewed and digested, actively consumed and interiorized. Even if at first it appears to be comprehensible and easily understandable – when we have finally taken it in, it can jolt us bitterly, destroy our inner tranquillity. Its message does not leave us indifferent; rather it occupies and involves us. It can pose unpleasant questions and challenge us to action.[20]

Paradoxically, it seems that while Scripture urges us to resist all the devil's efforts to persuade us to believe in the distorted, selective understandings of God that arise from a dominant theology that is legalistic and judgmental, it also calls us to beware of a superficially receptive, even 'joyful' response to God's word. Such a response grows out of a different dominant theology, another kind of partial and selective reading. We might characterize this as a triumphalist, 'Palm Sunday' kind of theology, the same understanding that the disciples on the Emmaus road and their surrounding culture had bought into. This theology builds on those Scriptures that justify a story about 'Jesus of Nazareth, who was a prophet mighty in deed and word before God and all the people ... the one to redeem Israel' but filters out the disturbing question, 'Was it not necessary that the Messiah should suffer these things?' (Luke 24:19, 21, 26).

A thoughtful and balanced article in *Christianity Today* highlights one aspect of this kind of selective theology:

> In countless venues throughout sub-Saharan Africa ... prosperity-tinged Pentecostalism is growing faster not just than other strands of Christianity, but than all religious groups, including Islam. Of Africa's 890 million people, 147 million are now 'renewalists' (a term that includes both Pentecostals and charismatics), according to a 2006 Pew Forum on Religion and Public Life study ... While Christians of all types and times have relied on God's material provision, the kind of blessings that such preachers often promise – such as divine expectations of abundant wealth, runaway professional success, and unassailable physical and emotional health – spring from a relatively recent, American brand of religious thought ... Once relegated to the periphery of American religious thought, the gospel of wealth now pierces the heart of Africa's dynamic, growing church ... And little wonder: a religion of hope gleams brightly against the bleak backdrop of African poverty ... In this climate teaching about the Cross and suffering can be unappealing.[21]

The gospel of wealth is not without its critics inside Africa. The article goes on to say:

> David Oginde, senior pastor of the 10,000-member Nairobi Pentecostal Church, believes he could triple his membership by promising wealth. 'But if that is all I am teaching, then I have lost the message,' he says. 'The kingdom of God is built on the Cross, not on bread and butter.' ... And Kenyan pastor David Muriithi ... laments the practice of promising people results. 'What if it does not happen?'[22]

Commenting on the phenomenon of the prosperity gospel, Christopher Wright notes that:

> While it is certainly true that material abundance can be a tangible
> sign of God's blessing, the link between the two is neither automatic
> nor reversible. That is to say, God calls for faith, obedience and ethical
> loyalty to the demands of the covenant *in bad as well as good times*.[23]

Which brings us back to the parable of the sower and the people Jesus
describes as those who 'when they hear the word receive it with joy. But …
they believe only for a while and in a time of testing fall away' (Luke 8:13).

'Some fell among thorns, and the thorns grew with it and choked it'
(Luke 8:7)

The 'lure of wealth' is also a specific aspect of the way Jesus helps his disciples
to imagine the third kind of terrain where the good seed falls among thorny
weeds (Matt. 13:22; Mark 4:19; Luke 8:14). In addition, the 'cares of the world'
compete to strangle the vulnerable new plant of the word. The outcome
recorded in Matthew and Mark is that in those people represented in this
category, the seed 'yields nothing' (Matt. 13:22; Mark 4:19) and in Luke, that
'their fruit does not mature' (Luke 8:14).

Zambian pastor and teacher Joe Kapolyo reflects on 'low-yield'
Christianity in his own context, in which the Western categories of 'sacred'
and 'secular', rooted in Enlightenment thinking, do not describe African
experience. 'The Enlightenment demands classification. But life for the
African must be embraced in its totality.'[24] Christianity came to Africa, not
only as a religion identified with alien colonial power, but also characterized
by a mindset that classified all of life into spiritual and secular and was
therefore foreign to traditional African spirituality in which these distinctions
do not function. Kapolyo proposes that, because of this, Christianity has
struggled to penetrate the inmost values of African culture, 'the inner person,
the deep culture that is the locus of the vision of life'.[25] Among these powerful
core African values Kapolyo cites, for example, commitment to the group, in
particular to the extended family and ethnic group:

> The experience of 'fellowship' in the natural family is so real and
> exclusive that it hinders and discourages fellowship in the church.
> The sense of solidarity stemming from common ancestry is so
> strong that it acts as a big barrier to the idea of extending the same
> sense of community to total strangers. Tribal churches thrive on this
> weakness.[26]

Perhaps one way of imagining those tough, strangling, thorny plants is as the powerful core values of 'deep culture' – whatever that culture may be and whatever its core values. Kapolyo warns us that,

> Ideally at conversion one would hope that it is the core values that are 'converted' and replaced by biblical values, derived from the Bible and enshrined in our hearts by the Holy Spirit … Fear, opportunities for commercial and political advancement, desire to create cohesion around a tribal identity, economic survival, all can play significant parts in the decision … to convert … it takes a long time before 'true' religion of the heart corresponds with what takes place at the expressive or surface level culture … This I believe is the reason why so often the church in Africa has been compared to a river two miles wide but a mere two inches deep![27]

Perhaps it is a healthy sense that our engagement with God's word is *not* addressing the core values of our cultures – those things that define us and make us who we are, and that are nevertheless challenged by the values of God's word – that prompts some of the moving and heartfelt responses that open this chapter: 'I simply don't experience the Bible as a place where God speaks to me'; 'I come to the Bible with low expectations of ever finding anything worthwhile there.' Joe Kapolyo writes about the urgent need for those who communicate God's word 'to be relevant to the African constituencies they serve. The repeating of evangelical platitudes originally conceived in other cultures will … not serve the African church.'[28] But this is surely not solely an African issue. David Smith quotes Helmut Thielicke's passionate critique of preaching in his day – that it involved 'the mere grinding out of a routine vocabulary – God, grace, sin, justification – which produces a kind of Christian gobbledegook that never gets under anybody's skin.' What is needed is 'the hard work and utter dedication of a new generation of prophetic teachers' who will help people to discover Scripture as utterly relevant for life today.[29]

Before you read further you might choose to spend some time reflecting on the comments that open this chapter. To what extent do you identify with any of them? Why not write down your own account of resistance to the word of God? How might this experience match one or more of the kinds of terrain that Jesus describes in his parable of the sower?

We have seen in chapter 1 how the living word of God can break through even the most hard-trodden paths of received doctrine and dominant theologies. David Bruce's story bears eloquent testimony to this hope. I want to end this chapter on another note of hope, with a story about resistance to God's word and the power of that word to bring about absolute transformation.

Dr Beyers Naudé was born in 1915 in the Transvaal. He was the son of an Afrikaner clergyman who was also a founding member of the secretive Broederbond, a group that played an active role in promoting the doctrine of apartheid in South Africa. Naudé followed in his father's steps to become a minister in the Dutch Reformed Church of South Africa (the NGK – Nederduits Gereformeerde Kerk – also referred to in English as the DRC). He also was an active member of the Broederbond until he resigned in 1963. He spent the first years of his ministry unquestioningly accepting the theology of apartheid. He had, after all, studied at Stellenbosch University under H. F. Verwoerd, one of the architects of the doctrine. In 1948, the Transvaal Synod of the NGK published a report entitled: 'Racial and national apartheid in Scripture'. This was the kind of doctrine that Naudé had grown to accept:

> The primary aim of the report was to show that segregation had to be deduced from Scripture as an imperative. The report therefore lumped together a large number of verses from Scripture without, however, any serious attempt to explain the exegetical validity of the enterprise. Merely quoting them was considered 'proof' of the obligatory nature of segregation. It was an example of profound fundamentalism.[30]

During his trial in 1973 for refusing to give evidence to the Schlebusch Commission (the Commission of Inquiry into Certain Organizations), Naudé gave an account of his experience of living with Scripture:

> I was born and brought up in a home where the reverence for the authority of the Bible served as foundation for our life and upbringing ... my father constantly emphasized the biblical and reformed truth of the sovereignty of God in all areas of human life, as also the necessity that the Christian should act correctly and justly, that these should be the foundation stones of the Christian's life. To the best of my ability ... I have tried to understand these convictions and truths and to live accordingly.[31]

Naudé explained that it was only when he started to work as an NGK chaplain at the University of Pretoria that the students' questions finally confronted him with the need to look again at his received worldview and its theological foundations:

> It was particularly in four different areas where I sought for light, based on the light of the Gospel. Firstly, the whole question of the unity and diversity of the human race; secondly on the unity and diversity of the Church on earth; thirdly, the responsibility of the Church in the different areas of human society, and, fourthly, the necessity for the Church to play the role of reconciler in situations of serious tension. Concerning the first, it became clear to me through this theological study ... that the traditional approach ... particularly that held by the three Afrikaans Churches, namely that the division of the human race is of primary concern, i.e., decisive, and that the unity is of secondary concern, i.e., subsidiary, that this was contrary to the insight of the Bible. I discovered that the truth of the Bible conveyed to us clearly that God created all the nations of the world in one blood, and that ... the unity of the human race is fundamental for the calling of man on earth.[32]

Later in his trial, in order to explain to the court why he had finally decided to pay the price of forfeiting his ministry with the NGK to take up the leadership of the multiracial Christian Institute, Naudé read out again the sermon he had preached to his congregation in Aasvoëlkop, Johannesburg, to explain his decision to them. As he started to read, standing in the witness box marked 'Whites', a storm of protest briefly silenced him. This is a taste of what he said:

> We bring you this morning the word of God from Acts 5:29 which reads as follows: 'We must obey God rather than men' and to understand what these words mean for the church and for society, but also for you and me we must first have a clear understanding of all that happened here [in Acts] ... By experience the Apostles now understand the truth of Scripture ... that the Gospel is a sign that will be contradicted – an experience of life into life and of death to death, a word that is alive and powerful and sharper than any two-edged sword ... You who together with us confess loyalty to Christ and his word, is your primary obedience and loyalty to Christ? Are you willing to call your people and your racial group to seek and to

put this obedience above all other things? Even when this clashes
with their deepest human sentiments?[33]

Along with other members of the Christian Institute Beyers Naudé was
'banned' under South African law between 1977 and 1984 and, after his trial,
briefly imprisoned. In the thirty years following his resignation from the
NGK, he worked covertly to support the anti-apartheid movement, though
he never became a member of the ANC. An excellent amateur mechanic, he
often provided vehicles for ANC fugitives.

In a conversation in 1985 with German theologian Dorothee Sölle,
Beyers Naudé described three of Carlos Mesters' 'factors external to the
text' (see page 14) that we have been considering in this chapter and that
prompted him to search the Scriptures. Firstly he became aware of deeply
disturbing parallels between what had happened in Nazi Germany and what
was happening in his own society. Secondly, he was becoming exposed to the
pain that apartheid laws were causing in the Transvaal, where young white
ministers were coming to him with the problems they were experiencing
within their African, Coloured and Indian congregations. 'And then they
invited me to go to their congregations ... and I was shattered. It was an
experience which led me to the situation of being totally lost.'[34]

For Naudé the final 'factor external to the text' was the Sharpeville
massacre in March 1960, when sixty-nine peaceful protesters were shot, most
in the back as they ran away from the police. 'And there was no way in which
I could get out of it any longer.'[35]

Beyers Naudé died in 2004, having returned in peace to his old
congregation in Johannesburg. At his funeral, the former archbishop of Cape
Town and fellow campaigner Desmond Tutu told the congregation that, 'Oom
Bey gave the credibility of Christianity back to black people.'[36]

The seed of the word of God, resisted for so long in Naudé's life as it
fell on the hard-trodden soil of racial prejudice, finally fell in 'good soil', soil
ploughed up by events and circumstances that had nothing directly to do
with the Bible text. But in that receptive ground the seed bore fruit.

3

God's Word

All Scripture is inspired by God and is useful ... for
training in righteousness
— 2 Timothy 3:16

Readers of this book will come with different expectations to a chapter on the authority of the Bible. For some of us, a discussion of the authority of Scripture and its nature as God's revelation may not seem to have much relevance. It is simply not an issue in our context. In large parts of Africa and Latin America many people have no difficulty in accepting the Bible as 'a book of devotion and norm of morality'.[37] Among Christian communities in these parts of the world, and especially among the poor, the Bible is, for the most part, unchallenged as God's trustworthy self-revelation. Carlos Mesters reports from Latin America that, 'the Bible is accepted by the people as the Word of God. They already have faith before they reach the stage of actually opening the Bible for the first time.'[38] At the same time, in Africa and Latin America and other parts of the world where the church played an active role in colonization, these same communities are often well aware that those holding political and ecclesiastical power have frequently invoked the authority of the Bible for their own unscrupulous ends. A popular saying in Southern Africa puts it like this: 'When the white man came to our country he had the Bible and we had the land. The white man said to us, "Let us close our eyes and pray." When we opened our eyes, the white man had the land and we had the Bible.' The misuse of Scripture to legitimize apartheid that we explored in the previous chapter sounds a further warning to us that to proclaim the authority of the Bible carries with it a heavy ethical responsibility.

An unquestioning trust in the Bible as God's word would also be true for many children, especially those brought up in a Christian home. In the same chapter cited in the epigraph for this chapter, Paul reminds his young disciple that 'from childhood you have known the sacred writings' (2 Tim. 3:15). Timothy was the child of a believing mother, and also had a believing grandmother (2 Tim. 1:5). Unless they have learned otherwise from adults, children are naturally trusting about the Bible and therefore vulnerable to manipulative or oppressive misuse of Scripture on the part of adults.

For many of us though, trust in the Bible as the authoritative word of God has come about gradually. We would identify with Ida Glaser's statement that, 'In fact, none of us *starts* by accepting God's revelation in Christ or in the Bible ... we need God to lead us to this understanding; and he leads us all in different ways.'[39] You might look back at the testimonies set out in chapter 1 and notice how some of these witnesses (Miltos Anghelatos and Nurat, for example) started out on their encounter with the Bible from a position of neutrality, curiosity or scepticism. They did not *begin* by accepting Scripture as God's authoritative word that sought a response from them. Rather, they discovered that authority *experientially*, interacting with what they read or heard, taking practical steps of obedience as they responded progressively to their understanding of what this word was saying to them, and discovering that God's word 'worked'. Implicit within each encounter is the unquantifiable, uncontrollable and mysterious activity of God's Holy Spirit.

A third group of us perhaps identify with the experience of the Cuban-American theologian Justo González. He writes frankly of his experience of the 'dry years' of seminary study and the notable academic achievements that followed. His knowledge and understanding of the Bible grew significantly in this time, but he 'no longer had any idea what to do with it'. He had slowly and imperceptibly lost the sense of engaging with God's word, not only to understand the historical context of a text but to explore its implications for living *today*.[40]

González describes two outcomes of what was happening:

> The first was that, just as my Bible studies, my preaching did not bring the Scripture closer to the people, but farther away ... The second consequence was that the whole issue of the authority of the Bible was a matter of much mystification for me, as well as for those whom I presumed to teach. I insisted on the authority of the Bible ... But it was really *a non-functioning authority* [my italics]. In truth authority lay in theology, in religious experience, and even in

religious and moral platitudes, and the Bible functioned only insofar as what it said agreed with these other authorities.[41]

Before reading further you might like to write down briefly your present understanding of the authority of the Bible. How have you reached that understanding? Do you believe it is adequate for today? You might want to consider these questions both in terms of your personal belief and in terms of how your Christian community thinks about the authority of Scripture.

As we seek to articulate our understanding of the Bible's authority, we may be challenged by Walter Brueggemann's statement that, 'Each generation of believers and scholars must answer its own particular form of the question of the authority of scripture, for the question is posed differently for different communities in different intellectual and cultural circumstances.'[42]

Through the centuries, Christian creeds and statements of belief have recognized the authoritative witness of the Bible.

- The fourth-century Nicene Creed affirms of Jesus that, 'On the third day he rose again in accordance with the Scriptures'.
- The 1646 Westminster Confession declares that, 'The authority of the holy Scripture, for which it ought to be believed and obeyed, dependeth not upon the testimony of any man or Church, but wholly upon God (who is truth itself), the Author thereof; and therefore it is to be received, because it is the Word of God.'[43]
- In 1965 the Second Vatican Council declared that, 'since everything asserted by the inspired authors or sacred writers must be held to be asserted by the Holy Spirit, it follows that the books of Scripture must be acknowledged as teaching solidly, faithfully and without error that truth which God wanted put into sacred writings for the sake of salvation.'[44]
- The 1974 Lausanne Covenant states: 'We affirm the divine inspiration, truthfulness and authority of both Old and New Testament Scriptures in their entirety as the only written word of God, without error in all that it affirms, and the only infallible rule of faith and practice. We also affirm the power of God's word to accomplish his purpose of salvation.'[45]

The intention of this chapter is to explore the basis on which Christians make these affirmations.

A story about authority

The Gospels of Matthew and Luke give us two accounts of a remarkable encounter in the lake town of Capernaum between Jesus and a middle-ranking Roman army officer (Matt. 8:5–13; Luke 7:1–10). At the heart of the story is the issue of authority. In Luke's account the centurion asks the Jewish leaders, with whom he has an excellent relationship, to plead with Jesus to come and heal his valued servant who is suffering from a distressing paralysis. For unspecified and intriguing reasons, the centurion has come to recognize this poor, itinerant teacher from Nazareth as a supreme authority ('Lord, I am not worthy to have you come under my roof; but only speak the word, and my servant will be healed'). Jesus sets out for the centurion's house, but (in Luke's version) before he can get there, the soldier's envoys meet him on the road with a message for him that is shaped by the centurion's experience of army life. He describes himself as 'a man under authority', constantly alert to orders. He in turn exercises authority through the commands he issues to his men: 'I say to one, "Go", and he goes, and to another, "Come", and he comes, and to my slave, "Do this", and the slave does it.' The centurion is prepared to trust that the word of Jesus, like his own commands to his men, is *a word that can rightly expect a response, a word that is able and intended to bring about action and change.* In an act of faith that astounds Jesus, the centurion throws himself on the authority of the Lord's word, clearly expecting an outcome of complete transformation (Matt. 8:7).

This deeply moving story offers us a helpful model as we think about the question of the authority of the Bible. At the heart of these accounts in Matthew and Luke is the identification by the army captain of the authority of the *word* with the authority of the *person* of Jesus. It is because the centurion recognizes Jesus to be 'Lord' and rightly in authority over him, that he acknowledges the power and trustworthiness of his word. For this Roman captain, because Jesus is who he is, his word does what it does.

Scripture is authoritative because it is the word of God

This same crucial process of identification of word with Person must take place in all of us if we are to interact with Scripture as an authoritative word for our lives. When we talk about 'the authority of Scripture' we are describing an authority that derives directly from the Person who makes himself known in the Bible, from his revelation of himself as God, Father, Son and Holy Spirit. N. T. Wright has written,

> The phrase 'authority of scripture' can only make Christian sense if it is a shorthand for 'the authority of the triune God, exercised somehow *through* scripture' ... it can only have any Christian meaning if we are referring to scripture's authority *in a delegated or mediated sense* from that which God himself possesses, and that which Jesus possesses as the risen Lord and Son of God.'[46]

The army officer in Capernaum gathered evidence about Jesus and checked the credentials of his authority in ways we can only guess at: from the reports of his Jewish contacts, perhaps from standing on the edge of a crowd listening to Jesus' teaching, perhaps from personally witnessing a healing. For us today, the Bible is our key resource for understanding what God is like and why we need to consider his claims of authority. As the Roman captain gathered evidence, we too need to gather evidence, to do what some of our 'witnesses' in chapter 1 did: set out, with as few preconceptions as possible, on a process of interaction with the Old and New Testaments. As we do so, we will find ourselves drawn in, from the opening words of Genesis, to a coherent and purposeful narrative. We will come face to face with the sovereignty of God whose authority is demonstrated at every point of the Bible's story. The word of this God in three Persons is *a word that rightly expects our response and has power to bring about action and change.* It is accomplishing the purposes of God, doing what God has sent it to do (Isa. 55:11). It is also a word that we can choose to resist, as we saw in the previous chapter. God's word is not a coercive word.

It seems to me that the kind of dry, discouraging experience of the Bible that Justo González describes comes about when our theoretical understanding of the authority of the Bible loses touch with our practice. Unlike the army captain in Capernaum we no longer *act on* and *live out* the word of Scripture because somehow we have lost the connection with the Person – the God who speaks to us. We no longer share his vision of kingdom and mission. In Justo González' words, this is a 'non-functioning authority'. David Smith probes this discontinuity between our theoretical assent to the authority of Scripture and our life experience:

> How has it happened that people who speak with such conviction and assurance about the atonement often show so little evidence in daily life, or in interpersonal relationships, of a 'crucified mind'?[47]

When the Bible becomes dry for us, or when we seek to evade its claims, we lose any impulse to grasp it and wrestle with it and test its trustworthiness. St Augustine's moment of sure faith came when he responded to a mysterious chanted invitation, apparently by a child, of the words, *'Tolle, lege! Tolle, lege!'* 'Pick up and read!'[48] The words in Romans 13:13, 14 that Augustine read that day went straight to the heart of his disordered life and pointed the way to radical change. Later, in a homily on John 8:37–47, he was to contrast his experience with that of the unbelieving Pharisees who rejected the authority of Jesus' words:

> Therefore He says, 'Ye seek to kill me, because my word taketh no hold in you.' If my word were taken, it would take hold: if ye were taken, ye would be enclosed like fishes within the meshes of faith. What then means that – 'taketh no hold in you'? It taketh not hold of your heart, because not received by your heart. For so is the word of God, and so it ought to be to believers, as a hook to the fish: it takes when it is taken.[49]

A surprising kind of authority

We are talking therefore about *God's authority articulated in, and worked out through, Scripture.* We understand that as we encounter the sovereign God who reveals himself to us in Scripture, he can rightly expect our response to his word. But how does this actually work out? What does it mean to seek to live under the authority of God 'exercised somehow *through* scripture'? N. T. Wright's use of the word 'somehow' implies that it is not always straightforward to understand and describe how this can be the case. The Bible is an entire library, not a single book. When we go to a library, we're aware that it contains texts of many different kinds. We would not describe all of them, by any means, in terms of their 'authority'. Take poetry, for example: we don't read a poem about the beauty of the stars on a winter night with the understanding that this text has *authority* over us in the same way that, say, the Highway Code requires us to behave on the road. We read or listen to poetry for its emotional power, for its creative beauty and perhaps because we sense that it expresses realities that we would like to put into words if only we could. If we choose to read a book on astrophysics, the concept of authority is perhaps clearer. We seek out a book by a respected scientist because we are reading to get reliable information.

The range of Scripture texts includes poems, songs, laws, genealogies, proverbs, riddles, letters, history, prophecy, stories, parables, apocalyptic writing. When we read Old Testament books such as Leviticus or Deuteronomy the idea of their 'authority' seems at first not to be problematic; they consist largely of laws and regulations. But in fact we *don't* live by these regulations today: Christians don't stone their rebellious sons to death (Deut. 21:18–21) or include animal sacrifice in their worship of God (Lev. 1). So in what way can we understand even these legal texts as authoritative? And what about the fact that so much of the Bible is narrative? How can we understand the story of the love between Ruth and Boaz to be authoritative for us? Or Paul's shipwreck? Or the poetry of the psalms? N. T. Wright expresses the problem with a couple of examples of apparently incongruous communication in a situation of authority:

> If the commanding officer walks into the barrack room and begins 'once upon a time', the soldiers are likely to be puzzled. If the secretary of the cycling club pins up a notice which, instead of listing times for outings, offers a short story, the members will not know when to turn up. At first sight, what we think of as 'authority' and what we know as 'story' do not readily fit together.[50]

But it only takes a little reflection for us to understand that the categories of story and song and poetry can in fact be authoritative because of their nature as powerful agents of change. Those soldiers may be puzzled initially by their officer's choice of a story to get them to act in a certain way. But his strategy is likely to take them by surprise, engage their imagination and make his orders unforgettable! Why else did Jesus so often tell stories in order to bring people face to face with their need to change? Why did the prophet Nathan choose to confront David with his sin through the medium of a story (1 Sam. 12:1–13)? Why is page after page of the Old Testament expressed as poetry? Because poetry and story can make us see things in new ways and engage us at deep levels of our being in ways that abstract, propositional material cannot do.[51] Walter Brueggemann warns us about our tendency in handling the Bible to flatten out and 'manage' the rich variety of its texts:

> The gospel is ... a truth widely held, but a truth greatly reduced ... flattened, trivialized, and rendered inane ... our technical way of thinking reduces mystery to problem, transforms assurance into

certitude, revises quality into quantity, and so takes the categories of biblical faith and represents them in manageable shapes.[52]

We are not to 'manage' the Bible's rich variety of writing, reducing it to abstract principles, but delight in its variety and respond to all the surprising ways in which we experience its power to bring about change in us.

We need to be aware that people in different cultures are likely to think in different categories about different genres of writing and how their authority is perceived. In his book on the history and role of the Bible in Africa, Ype Schaaf writes about the importance of stories for the understanding of biblical values. He imagines asking a village elder what he thinks 'goodness' is. The old man, rich in life experience, will tell a long story. *This* is what goodness looks like, how it acts and speaks and relates. No abstract propositions, but a *story* about a person. Schaaf describes how the old man may struggle with non-narrative biblical material (non-narrative in form, at least):

> The Epistles of Paul will not say much to him. They will not touch him … Christ, the goodness of God become an ordinary man, … will speak to him and so will … the Acts of the Apostles. He will be on home ground with people of flesh and blood like Peter, John the Baptist and Zacchaeus. He appreciates the stories of the patriarchs in the Old Testament … he recognises his own proverbs in the book of Ecclesiastes. The parables remind him of his own fables that end with a moral. The struggle with God of which the Psalms speak, through joy and sorrow, in distress and deliverance, is a struggle that is real in his own life.[53]

What is happening here? The African believer who engages with the Bible, rather than standing back and analyzing the text, actually discovers most of it to be home ground, a narrative in which he participates and recognizes his own experience. In short, it is 'his story'. Western Christians, on the other hand, belonging to a culture that has tended to marginalize story and place greater emphasis on logical, rational thought, often strain to bridge the gap between the world of the Bible and their own world and to work out how to 'apply' Scripture to their lives. The African dynamic is described by Justo González from a Latin American perspective: 'We read the Bible, not primarily to find out what we are to do, but to find out who we are and who we are to be.'[54] Carlos Mesters writes about the informal Catholic Bible discussion groups in Brazil, 'The Bible is no longer seen as a rather strange book belonging only to the clergy, but as *our* book, "written for us until the end of time" (1 Cor. 10:11).'[55]

Engaging with the Bible for transformation

We talked earlier about the Bible as a coherent and purposeful narrative, characterized by the authoritative words and actions of its central character, God himself. But we can engage with the Bible in ways that domesticate it and somehow tame its power to be authoritative in our lives. We then miss its dynamic interaction with us in bringing about the kingdom of God, working out God's purposes in this world.

For example, we can read the Bible merely *as a source of information*. We reduce the rich and complex texts of Scripture to a set of systematized descriptions about God. But we have no sense that these descriptions make claims of us. We're back to that sense of a 'non-functioning authority'. We can also read Scripture *in a piecemeal way*, rarely straying beyond those passages that are familiar and comforting or that fit our cultural preferences. The Western Christian may need encouragement to engage with Leviticus or Ezekiel; the African village elder should not miss out on Paul's letters! If we engage only with our preferred texts, we will lose sight of the coherent story of God's purposes and are also likely to miss some crucial interaction with unfamiliar passages that can take us by surprise. An *overly personal, individual engagement* with God's word can also enable us to evade the claims of God's word on our lives, so that all our theory of the authority of Scripture is neutered. It becomes a non-functioning authority. It's important that we balance our personal engagement with God's word with regular engagement *in community* so that our prejudices are questioned and our blind spots revealed.

Exploring the Bible's 'inspiration'

The statements of belief about the Bible that we listed on page 29 refer to some important ideas that underpin Christian belief in the authority of the Bible. The Westminster Confession talks of God as 'the Author' of Scripture; the Vatican document refers to the Bible's 'inspired authors' and the interaction of the Holy Spirit with them; the Lausanne Covenant affirms the Bible's 'divine inspiration'. The Bible says very little about itself, how it came into being or what its inspired nature means. It is far more concerned to draw us into the story of God. However, two brief New Testament passages do refer to the dual authorship of Scripture. The second letter attributed to Peter describes the dynamic interaction of human authors and divine Author: 'No prophecy ever came by human will, but men and women moved by the Holy Spirit spoke from God' (2 Pet. 1:21). And Paul, reminding Timothy of how important 'the sacred writings' have been in the development of his faith, focuses on why these writings continue to be an unfailing resource for living God's way. Their power lies in their inspiration by God himself (2 Tim. 3:16). (We should note that the translation of this verse is debatable. It can be read as 'All scripture is inspired by God and is useful' or as 'Every scripture inspired by God is also useful' [NRSV footnote] or 'All inspired scripture has its use' [REB].)

I wonder how you think about and imagine the Bible as 'inspired'? There are several different ways in which people describe how they understand it.[56] We will briefly outline three of these.

- A 'divine dictation' or 'prophetic' understanding of biblical inspiration. In the Old Testament God's word often comes to the prophet in a dream or as an inner voice. Jeremiah said, 'The word of the Lord came to me' (Jer. 32:6); 'the word of the Lord came by the prophet Haggai' (Hag. 1:1); 'at that time the Lord had spoken to Isaiah son of Amoz' (Isa. 20:2). The prophet communicates God's message to the people and in time the message is written down for wider use. Some people apply this way of understanding inspiration to the whole of the Bible, insisting that it is *all* the result of a kind of hot line from God to the Bible authors. They ask, for example, how Luke could have known the contents of the tribune's letter to Felix (Acts 23:25–30) or how the author of Genesis could have known about the Garden of Eden if God did not directly inform them. The problem with this concept of inspiration is that it does not reflect the way other biblical writers seem to have understood their role. Far from being passive receivers of the dictated word of God, they often refer to a normal human process of recording events and drawing on resources available to them. For example, Luke describes the research for his Gospel (Luke 1:1–4) and John refers to other accounts of Jesus' activities that he is aware of (John 21:25).
- A 'great literature' understanding of biblical inspiration. This is at the opposite end of the scale from the 'divine dictation' theory. It attributes any inspiration in the Bible firmly to the human authors, brilliant

artists and wordsmiths whose poetry and stories can grip and move us. It discounts any participation by God in the creation of Scripture. The Bible understood in this way has little or no prophetic significance for our lives today. It is the work of human authors, much of it of outstanding literary worth

- A 'concursive' understanding of biblical inspiration. This approach understands the normal human literary processes of research, use of available records, collecting and editing of documents to *concur* with the unseen activity of God's Holy Spirit at every stage of the human process. In the same way that many Christians understand the creation of the universe both as a process that can be described in scientific terms of cause and effect *and* as a result of the creative activity of God, so we can hold together our understanding of the Bible as the result of divine and human interaction. But even this understanding does not explain exactly how the Bible was 'inspired'.

> The doctrine of inspiration is a declaration that the Scriptures have their origin in God; it is not and cannot be an explanation of how God brought them into being ... In the end, therefore, it is a matter of faith whether we accept the hypothesis of the divine inspiration of Scripture ... it is the result of the working of the Spirit in our minds to initiate and sustain faith.[57]

The importance of biblical scholarship

In many parts of the world it is difficult and expensive to get hold of good literature to help us to engage with the Bible and keep up to date on debates about interpretation, authority and inspiration. The Internet can be a useful resource if we are selective and wise about the websites we consult. It is important that we try to grow in our understanding of God's word, exploring how we can engage with it and enable others to do so. Wherever we live in the world, if we have access to libraries, to scholars, to the rich resources available to us via the Internet, we should make use of them. For example, the exciting account of how the Bible came into being is beyond the scope of this book. But we can find it on the websites of various Bible Societies around the world. We should inform ourselves too about how the 'canon' of the Old and New Testaments came to its present shape (for Protestant Christians) of sixty-six books. Appendix 1 on page 143 lists some of these websites and helpful books.

In the next chapter we will look at another aspect of the authority of the Bible: the question of how we interpret it and understand it to address us today in the context of our cultures. I want to close this rather theoretical chapter with one of Eugene Peterson's memorable stories. Anthony was a truck driver in Peterson's congregation. He had never read a book but in the year after becoming a Christian he read the King James Bible three times. His wife Mary, intrigued by the change in him, often asked him questions about the Bible. Sometimes he needed advice and would invite the pastor round to their trailer home. One day Peterson was trying to help Mary understand the parables and found himself floundering. Anthony broke in, 'Mary, you got to live 'em, then you'll understand 'em; you can't figger 'em out from the outside, you got to git inside 'em – or let them git inside you.'[58] To trust Scripture as the word of God, to subscribe to its authority, involves us in *living* that word, as the centurion lived out his trust in the word of Jesus, as Nurat and Miltos Anghelatos tested and proved the word they had heard. It can't be figured out from the outside.

4

Interpreted Word

*No prophecy of scripture
is a matter of one's own interpretation*
— 2 Peter 1:20

'A re you saying that God speaks through the Bible only when we've got all our interpretational principles right?' The sudden question came from my Jamaican colleague, the late, much loved Gene Denham.

We were coming to the end of a workshop on interpreting Scripture and relating it to our lives. Wanting to illustrate the importance of the context of any Bible passage, I told the group about a sermon I'd heard recently in a Bolivian church. The preacher spoke on the parable of the Good Samaritan (Luke 10:25–37), explaining it in terms that I found unacceptable. The Good Samaritan was Jesus, he said; the injured man represented humanity, wounded by sin. The oil and wine with which the Samaritan cleaned and dressed the man's wounds symbolized the blood of Jesus, poured out to cleanse human sin. The preacher made no mention of the lawyer's question, 'And who is my neighbour?' that provides the immediate context for Jesus' story.

'And a lot of people in the congregation seemed to be deeply moved by his sermon – that's what I found so surprising!' My arrogant comment to the group prompted the question from Gene that brought me up short. I've always been grateful to her for asking a question that's kept me thinking and exploring ever since!

The preacher whose sermon I described had been following (perhaps unconsciously) an ancient tradition of literary interpretation, found especially in the work of Origen (c.AD185–254), one of the greatest biblical scholars of the third-century church. Origen explained Jesus' parable like this in one of his homilies:

> The man who was going down is Adam. Jerusalem is paradise, and
> Jericho is the world. The robbers are hostile powers. The priest is the
> Law, the Levite is the prophets, and the Samaritan is Christ. The wounds
> are disobedience ... the [inn], which accepts all who wish to enter, is
> the Church ... The manager of the [inn] is the head of the Church,
> to whom its care has been entrusted. And the fact that the Samaritan
> promises he will return represents the Saviour's second coming.[59]

Was the preacher mistaken in following Origen's example in interpreting Jesus'
parable to his congregation? If so, why? Or was I wrong to be critical of him?
What do we make of Gene's question about 'interpretational principles'? In
this chapter we explore some of the issues and questions around the complex
theme of biblical interpretation or 'hermeneutics' and why hermeneutics
matters so much when we engage with the Bible.

What is 'hermeneutics'?

'Hermeneutics' is the technical word used to describe the science and art
of interpretation, especially of sacred texts. Hermeneutics can be thought
of as scientific because of the development over time of certain guidelines
or principles of interpretation; it can also be thought of as an art because
exploring the meaning of a text doesn't depend solely on rigidly applying those
rules or principles. In chapter 7 we will explore how children develop a sense
of the meaning of the world that surrounds them. When a child interacts with
God's word, many different elements contribute at different developmental
stages to making a Bible story 'meaningful' (or not) for him or her. These
elements start with simple enjoyment and continue through emotional and
imaginative interaction with the Bible to the more sophisticated processes of
working out the personal implications and the context of what he is reading
or hearing (see pages 99–113). This same range of factors is in play when
people of any age explore the meaning for them of aspects of their world,
including the meaning of the Bible.

'Hermeneutics' derives from the Greek *hermeneuō*, to interpret. The
origin of the word is unknown, though it has been suggested that it may
be related to the name of the god Hermes who in Greek mythology acted
as a messenger or mediator between human beings and the remote gods,
interpreting the actions and words of the gods to humans. Hermeneutics
'involves the careful and creative use of various reading strategies aimed at

bridging the gulf between ancient scriptural texts and the modern reader … biblical interpretation has the goal of making it possible for God's people to hear God's word afresh, in idioms which contemporary men and women understand, but which are also faithful to the biblical witness.'[60]

Hermeneutics through history

Hermeneutics is not a new discipline. It is fascinating to explore how people have interpreted the Jewish and Christian Scriptures through the centuries. This kind of research can help us to understand some of the issues and tensions in our own experience of interpreting the Bible. We discover that from earliest times interpreters of Scripture have not gone about their work in a cultural vacuum; they have been influenced by the trends and issues of their times – philosophical, political and theological – as we too are influenced by our contexts as we interpret the Bible today. A complete survey of biblical interpretation is beyond the scope of this book. But we can consider a few significant turning points in the story.

Third-century Alexandria was a wealthy and cultured city where Greek philosophy, especially the ideas of Plato, deeply influenced Jewish and Christian scholars. Allegorical understandings – 'the belief that above and beyond the literal meaning of the text there stands a higher (or perhaps several higher) senses'[61] – held sway. When Philo, a Jewish philosopher and interpreter of the Hebrew Scriptures, explained the Pentateuch, he followed Plato's allegorical approach to interpreting, for example, Homer's poems. Philo was concerned to demonstrate to Alexandria's Greek intelligentsia that the Jewish Scriptures, when interpreted in this way, offered insights that were as valid as anything in Greek philosophy. We could describe his intentions as apologetic and evangelistic; he wanted to commend the Hebrew Scriptures to the pagan Greeks. As we have seen in his sermon on the parable of the Good Samaritan, Origen, also a citizen of Alexandria, followed this allegorizing trend.

But the tradition of allegorical interpretation had plenty of critics. Towards the end of the fourth century, Syrian Antioch became the focus of a hermeneutical tradition that rejected allegory as a valid interpretational approach, and began to take seriously the historical context of a Bible text. The school of Antioch taught that God had revealed himself in history and that the Bible was the coherent story of his salvation intentions. One of the key tasks of the interpreter was therefore to explain textual difficulties with reference to the historical context.[62]

With the Reformation in the sixteenth century came acknowledgment that allegorical understandings and 'literal', historically based readings of Scripture might *both* be valid. What mattered was that the interpretive approach should be faithful to the intentions of the biblical author. One of the factors in Luther's break with Roman Catholicism was his realization that this tradition relied greatly on authoritarian and often fanciful allegorizing that excluded lay people from meaningful engagement with God's word. Luther provided two further important dimensions to the understanding of biblical interpretation. He insisted that the aim of all reading and interpreting of Scripture is to meet with and understand the person of Jesus Christ, whose reality pervades the entire biblical record. Luther also emphasized the importance of human experience in interpreting the Bible: 'Experience is necessary for the understanding of the Word. It is not merely to be repeated or known, but to be lived and felt.'[63] Reacting against what he regarded as the shifting sands of the allegorical tradition, Luther also proposed that any Bible passage must have a single meaning: 'I consider the ascription of several senses to Scripture to be not merely dangerous and useless for teaching but even to cancel the authority of Scripture whose meaning ought always to be one and the same.'[64]

Five centuries after Luther, in those cultures that we describe as 'postmodern', the idea of 'one and the same' meaning for any text, including the text of Scripture, has come under powerful critical scrutiny. The influential French philosopher Jacques Derrida (1930–2004) proposed that, 'To ask a reader to conform to the "proper" meaning of the text is … a form of oppression, the same kind of oppression that pretends there is a "proper" way to dress or a "proper" way to paint.'[65] There are real tensions, even within evangelical Christianity, between these two approaches to seeking meaning and truth in Scripture:

> Two contrasting interpretations of interpretation now compete for the soul of Western culture. One seeks to decipher and to locate a stable determinate meaning; the other affirms the free play of signs … The one seeks understanding; the other tries to avoid being taken in.[66]

Similar tensions can also be discerned in the global South, where the Bible is increasingly read and interpreted in different ways. In the rest of this chapter we will explore what kind of guidelines may help us as we come to God's word and – inevitably – interpret it.

Hermeneutics and communication

Interpretation is an unavoidable aspect of communication. Every day we encounter many different kinds of communication. We read newspapers, magazines, novels and computer manuals, view websites, watch television, films and advertisements, listen to instructions, information, conversations and jokes. When we hear or read words or see images and signs, we interpret them, seeking their meaning and implications for us. The extent to which we engage with, understand and respond to any example of communication will vary greatly, depending on a wide range of different factors: our familiarity with the language used, whether we perceive the communication as relevant to us, interesting, inspiring or important, our opinion of the person or organization that is communicating, how the message resonates with our life experience, and so on.

Dr Melba Maggay from the Philippines tells a story about her first visit to Britain: 'I was a bit apprehensive because it was a strange land and I had no friends there. As a student I had very little money. If I ran out of money there was nobody to borrow from. But then on the first billboard I saw coming out of the airport were the words TAKE COURAGE! "Oh," I said, "that's very edifying. It's good that the British welcome me with this message!" Of course I learned afterwards that Courage is a brand of beer!'[67]

As we saw in the last chapter, one of the cornerstones of Christian belief is that God addresses us in Scripture. The Bible is a message that from start to finish seeks our response. Dr Maggay's experience demonstrates that in order to *respond* appropriately to any message we need to *interpret and understand* it. The message TAKE COURAGE! could be interpreted in different ways. In fact UK advertisers created it to be a deliberately ambiguous joke. Because Dr Maggay was new to the culture of British beer advertising, she understood the message at first only as friendly encouragement to visitors. This was not a serious misunderstanding but it illustrates how communication can fail or only function partially, especially when it seeks to speak across cultures.

Cross-cultural communication in the Bible

The Bible, as we saw in the last chapter, is a library of texts that communicate to us across a vast time span and from different cultural perspectives. As we get to know this library, we will form opinions about the ease or difficulty of understanding different parts of the Bible. Some passages will seem very clear to us. For example, the commandments 'You shall not murder' (Exod. 20:13) or 'Fathers, do not provoke your children to anger, but bring them up in the discipline and instruction of the Lord' (Eph. 6:4) appear to fall into this category. Other texts will be more like the advertisement that Dr Maggay *thought* was clear and to which she responded, but which in fact needed an explanation for its full cultural implications to be understood. For example, when we read in Luke 19:2 that Zacchaeus was a wealthy 'chief tax-collector' we may *partly* understand the crowd's angry reaction and accusation that Jesus had gone 'to be the guest of one who is a sinner' (v. 7). But in order fully to grasp the implications of this passage we will need to learn how deeply the Jewish people hated tax-collectors as collaborators with the Romans.

Our perceptions about what is familiar and easily understandable in the Bible will also vary according to our cultural contexts. For example, many Western people find large parts of the Old Testament difficult to understand and relate to their experience. There seems to be little common ground. Meanwhile, the indigenous peoples of the global South often discover that these texts describe ways of life and thought that are familiar to them. They may recognize in the Genesis accounts their own creation narratives and stories of the beginnings of the human race; the Old and New Testament genealogies are likely to feel familiar to them because of the importance of ancestors in their cultures. On the other hand the New Testament letters and the Gospels may be easier for Western people to relate to than the book of Revelation that takes them into a category of communication that is usually unfamiliar to them. We should be cautious about taking such preferences for granted though. No group of people is homogenous and many today in the West rebel against the rationalism of modernity and seek a renewal of the imaginative faculty.

We can expect the Bible to communicate; we can also expect the Bible to provoke different understandings

Two key facts begin to emerge as we consider communication in general, how the Bible communicates to us, and how we understand it and respond to it. The first fact is that the people who generated the Bible writings intended and expected their work to express something understandable to readers or listeners and to elicit responses that were appropriate to the message they sought to communicate. 'The underlying presupposition of the story of Israel, and the story of humanity as a whole, is that humans are able to understand the Word of God and words in general.'[68]

The second fact is that the Bible, like other texts and means of communication, provokes *different* understandings and responses, depending on who is reading or listening to it. People may disagree or differ about their understandings of the Bible. One reason for this is that because of our cultural and theological contexts and emphases and our life experience, we can often grasp hold of *one* aspect of the Bible and treat it as if this were the *whole*. A familiar Asian story illustrates this memorably. Some blind men were asked to describe what an elephant was like. One of them began feeling the elephant's side. He thought it must be like a wall. Another got hold of the tusk; it was sharp and pointed and he thought an elephant must be like a sword. A third man got hold of the ear. 'An elephant must be like a fan,' he said. Another man got hold of the legs and said, 'This is like a tree trunk.' In one sense all the blind men were accurate in their understanding of what an elephant was like. It *did* feel like a tree, like a fan, like a sword or a wall. But none of them was entirely correct because each understood a *part* of the elephant as if it were the *whole*.

Dr Maggay suggests that Western Christians have traditionally emphasized the doctrine of sin and grace and handled it as if it were the *whole* Bible story. In contrast, liberation theology in Latin America has focused on issues of God's love for the poor and his concern for social justice, while African and Filipino theologies often concentrate on God as Lord over the spirit world.[69] In fact no one of these emphases, on its own, is adequate to describe what the Bible is about. We all need to become aware of our particular blind spots. Otherwise we will neglect the unfailing richness of Scripture and its power to address all of life.

In summary, it is God's intention and expectation and promise to communicate to us through his word. But as we saw in chapter 2, we can have serious blind spots and prejudiced cultural understandings that make us resist that word, or undervalue and even deny other people's perceptions of Scripture. Jesus challenged the Pharisees to let their knowledge of Scripture change their behaviour, to move from knowing to doing, from ritual to compassionate action (Matt. 9:10–13). How then can we seek to make sure that we are reading or listening to Scripture with integrity and in ways that open us up to the transforming power of God's word? We move on now to explore practical ways in which we can work at this crucially important task. We start by what we all inevitably bring to any interaction with God's word – our worldview.

Our worldviews shape our response to Scripture

Nata, a Panamanian Chocó Indian Christian and wife of the pastor of the recently established church, was seriously ill. The Western missionary working among her people had some medical training and recognized the symptoms of pneumonia. He was deeply troubled, partly because he knew there were no antibiotics available, but more so because he was reading the letter of James in his daily time of prayer and Bible reflection. He had just read in chapter 5, 'Are any among you sick? They should call for the elders of the church and have them pray over them, anointing them with oil in the name of the Lord. The prayer of faith will save the sick, and the Lord will raise them up' (Jas. 5:14, 15). The missionary debated with himself, certain that if the believers knew about the passage, they would do exactly what it said, but aware that his own worldview made it difficult for him to say anything. He knew about pneumonia, he knew that antibiotics would cure Nata. But he questioned how the Spirit of God might destroy the infection.

His conscience wouldn't allow him to keep silent, so he wrote out a translation of the passage in James, handed it to Nata's husband, the pastor, and went into the forest to pray. When he returned some time later the pastor met him, desperate to know what oil they should use to anoint his wife: castor oil, motor oil or a little olive oil that some doctor had left behind. The pastor had already called the church elders who formed a circle with the missionaries around his sick wife. They prayed and laid hands on her. It became immediately clear that she was better, though not fully healed. The missionary felt relieved: 'So far, so good! At least it had not been a flop!'

But the next day brought grim news. Nata had got worse during the night and was more seriously ill than ever. The missionary was aware that the pastor had again sent for the church elders. They gathered once more to pray and lay hands on Nata. But this time no one sent for the missionary or asked his advice. And this time Nata was fully healed.

Later that day, as Nata took up her normal life and cooked for her family, the missionary approached the pastor and commented on the healing. The pastor expressed his joy at the Lord's goodness and the Holy Spirit's power. The missionary tentatively mentioned the lack of an invitation to pray with the elders the second time. He was devastated when the pastor told him they had not felt able to invite him back because they were aware that he didn't believe, and to have unbelievers included in prayer invalidated the healing.

As he reflected on what had happened, the missionary came to understand how deeply his worldview shaped his reading of and response to Scripture. He saw how the Chocó believers understand the Spirit of God to be central in all matters related to healing, and how in response to this understanding, prayer and medicine (when available) are always offered *together* for a sick person. Their understanding of both is profoundly integrated. The missionary wrote: 'My culture, with its complete separation between the material and the spiritual, was robbing me of the capacity to believe.' He then added, 'Thoughtful Christians must be honestly aware of both their own worldview ... and that of the Bible.'[70]

When Jesus preached in the Nazareth synagogue on a text from Isaiah he claimed that his congregation was now witnessing the text's true meaning and fulfilment. As he went on to challenge the people's complacency by quoting examples of Israel's rejection of the prophets and of God's choice of people outside Israel such as Naaman, the people rose in fury against him. Their worldview of themselves as God's privileged people clashed head-on with Jesus' understanding of the global scope of God's dealings with humanity and his prophetic perception of how these Nazareth people would finally reject him (Luke 4:16–30).

As we come to explore ways in which we can seek to read and understand Scripture with integrity and true openness, the first thing we need to grasp is that we all, without exception, encounter the Bible with a certain worldview, through a series of cultural lenses. There is no such thing as a 'neutral' reading of Scripture. Every reading is inevitably an interpretation shaped by a worldview:

> Anyone who has worked within biblical scholarship knows, or ought to know ... that integrity consists not of having no presuppositions but of being aware of what one's presuppositions are and of the obligation to listen and to interact with those who have different ones.[71]

We've just witnessed four worldviews that prompted four different responses to Scriptures – from the Chocó believers, the Western missionaries, the Jewish people gathered in the Nazareth synagogue, and Jesus himself. We are already implying that the Chocó believers' response to the letter of James and Jesus' interpretation of Isaiah and other passages in the Old Testament, reflect a more *faithful* understanding and interpretation of Scripture than the missionary's hesitant and doubting understanding or the racially superior understanding of the Nazareth congregation. In this chapter we will explore what we can do to try to make sure that our understanding of Scripture is not so influenced by our context and worldview that it becomes unfaithful and unfruitful.

Understanding our own worldview

A great range of factors shape our worldview. They include our gender and age, our nationality and ethnic identity, the history of our people group or nation, our level of education, rural or urban background, religious affiliation and the expectations and norms of the surrounding society in matters such as family, sex and sexuality, work, leisure, attitudes to old age, youth, children, death, authority, hierarchy, power, wealth and poverty, understandings of beauty and creativity. Our worldview as Christians may be further shaped by our denominational affiliation and theological traditions.

Before reading further in this chapter you might like to take time to build up a picture of your own worldview so as to become more aware of how it influences all your interaction with the Bible. You could fill in the grid below and add comments as you become aware of different aspects of your worldview and their impact on how you respond to God's word. I have found that it's even better to do this exercise with a friend from another culture!

Worldview influences	Description of myself	How might this impact on my understanding of Scripture?
Your age		
Your gender and personality (e.g. introvert, extrovert; whether you are mainly a 'thinking' person or a 'feeling' person)		
Married, single, widowed, divorced		
Nationality/ethnicity		

Worldview influences	Description of myself	How might this impact on my understanding of Scripture?
History of your nation		
Language(s)		
Education		
Rural / urban background		
Religion / denomination		
Key life experiences – both joyful and painful		
Economic situation		
How does your cultural context influence your attitudes to: family sex and sexuality work time health and sickness old age youth / children death authority and power hierarchy wealth and poverty beauty and creativity other peoples and nations the Christian church the Bible people of other faiths		
What do you think are the core values of your culture? (see Chapter 2, p. 22)		
What is your favourite book in the Bible? Why do you think this is so?		
Which is your least favourite book in the Bible? Why do you think this is so?		

Understanding the place of interpretation in understanding and responding to God's word

Dr Maggay's partial understanding of the message TAKE COURAGE! was eventually completed. Someone interpreted the message to her by explaining its context as an advertisement. Now she not only felt encouraged but also understood the other meaning of the message and could choose how to respond to its invitation!

The task of interpreting, of explaining Scripture, is as old as the Scriptures themselves. For example, the book of Nehemiah presents us with a memorable scene in which Ezra and other leaders 'read from the book, from the law of God, with interpretation. They gave the sense so that the people understood the reading' (Neh. 8:8). The reading and interpretation, which probably included an element of translation of unfamiliar Hebrew words, provoked an initial response of powerful grief and repentance and then one of joy. 'All the people went their way … to make great rejoicing, because they had understood the words that were declared to them' (Neh. 8:12). Eugene Peterson comments that the outcome of faithful interpretation is to 'bring about the kind of understanding that involves the whole person in tears and laughter, heart and soul, in what is written, what is said.'[72] In Luke 4:16–30 we listen to Jesus reading and interpreting passages from Isaiah and other parts of the Old Testament. We hear him refer to how Elijah and Elisha related to people outside the Jewish community. He treats these narratives as reliable history. But he doesn't stop at reading and expounding what happened *then*. He relates these texts to the people listening in the synagogue *now*. 'Today this scripture has been fulfilled in your hearing,' he says of Isaiah's words from centuries before. And, 'Doubtless you will quote to me this proverb, "Doctor, cure yourself!"' He makes it clearly understood that the people in the synagogue now are behaving just like the Jewish people who rejected Elijah and Elisha then, despising God's spokesmen. His interpretation of Scripture is a warning that provokes a response of fury.

Over the centuries the church has developed principles for interpreting the Bible. In the examples we have looked at earlier in this chapter of trends in interpretation, we can see that at different times, different principles have received more or less emphasis. We now explore one attempt to provide guidelines that have been prepared for, and evaluated by, an international constituency.[73]

Principles for faithful interpretation of the Bible

The Bible should be interpreted:

- **Prayerfully,** in humility and in dependence on the Holy Spirit
- **Corporately** rather than individualistically
- **As a whole,** allowing Scripture to interpret Scripture, and seeking to understand the broad sweep of God's dealings with humanity from creation to new creation
- **Contextually – as it was written,** acknowledging the Bible's different literary forms and seeking to understand the author's intention and the historical and canonical context of a passage
- **Contextually – as it is encountered.** Every encounter is an interpretation. While our communities exercise a significant influence on our understanding of Scripture, they are not ultimately a binding force. We need constantly to bring our understanding of Scripture back to Scripture. At the same time we need to listen to the interpretation of Scripture of others, so that our understanding may be enriched and our blind spots corrected.
- **Contextually – as it is lived out.** Encountering God through his word will have an impact on our lives, encouraging us in worship, mission, and holiness.
- **Christologically.** Jesus Christ (his birth and life on earth, his death and resurrection, his ascension and second coming) is God's key Word in his dealings with human beings; and he, therefore, is the focus of God's revelation in the Bible.
- **Relationally.** We do not read the Bible simply to collect information about God. Rather, through the stories, promises, commands, warnings and examples, we begin to understand God, meet with him and know him personally.

We go on now to explore these principles more deeply.

The Bible should be interpreted prayerfully

It's impossible to exaggerate the importance of prayer as the primary context for all our engagement with the Bible. In the Nehemiah 8 narrative, prayer and worship precede and follow the reading of the Scriptures. Ezra and the people bless the Lord, bow down in worship and later respond to Scripture in prayers of confession. The Scriptures of both Old and New Testaments provide words for us to express our need of the Holy Spirit to understand God's word: 'To you, O Lord, I lift up my soul ... in you I trust ... Make me to know your ways, O Lord; teach me your paths' (Ps. 25:1, 2, 4). Jesus invites us to 'Ask ... search ... knock' so that we may discover that closed doors open because 'how much more will the heavenly Father give the Holy Spirit to those who ask him!' (Luke 11:9–13).

My own experience of writing resources to help people engage with Scripture has taught me how easy it is to come to rely on commentaries and a store of memorable quotations. Time and again I have experienced how a Bible passage remains lifeless and almost meaningless, even with all the help of commentators and creative techniques, until I acknowledge to God in often desperate prayer that I can write nothing worthwhile without the help of his Holy Spirit. As I admit my powerlessness, connections and convictions will mysteriously come to mind – sometimes slowly and laboriously, and sometimes like a lightning strike – that I know are not of my own making. I recognize the Spirit's creative power to make something new in bringing together God's word and the realities and needs of the people for whom I write.

> The Holy Spirit did not act just once through the authors who wrote the holy Scriptures. The Spirit still acts in persons who read the Scriptures, and only the Spirit's presence can ensure that the letter of Scripture will be constantly freshened and renewed to become spirit for the reader. The Scriptures become the life-giving Word only when God's Spirit energizes the person reading them.[74]

The Bible should be interpreted corporately rather than individualistically

Scripture communicates to us a strong sense of a *community* listening and responding to God's word. We've already heard Ezra reading and explaining Scripture to the gathered exiles, and Jesus reading and interpreting Isaiah in the synagogue. On the day of Pentecost Peter interprets Joel and Psalms 16 and 110 to the Jerusalem crowds as words that make sense of recent events (Acts 3:12–26). The Beroean Jewish community eagerly examine the Scriptures together to evaluate the preaching of Paul and Silas (Acts 17:10, 11). Paul's letters are publicly read among the young churches (Col. 4:16; 1 Thess. 5:27). Such communal reading ensures that individual blind spots and prejudices can be corrected by the understandings of others. It also, crucially, encourages and enables obedient response.

The corporate interpretation of Scripture has several dimensions to it. The community of the church has a *chronological* dimension. As we have seen earlier in this chapter, in considering hermeneutical development down the centuries, we can access documents that show us how the Christians of the first centuries were reading and understanding Scripture, how the medieval church and the Reformation scholars did so, and how Scripture is faring today in a context of globalization. At the 2006 meeting of the Forum of Bible Agencies International in Thailand, the leadership team presented a survey of interpretations of the book of Ruth from the fourth century to the present day. In the late medieval period, for example, the French scholar Nicholas of Lyra wrote on what he termed the 'moral sense' of chapter 2:

> In this chapter Ruth goes humbly and diligently into Boaz's field, gleaning grain. The field signifies sacred Scripture, which is a field full of the best knowledge and sense, just like good fruit; and for this reason it is the field which the Lord blesses ... The harvesters who belong to the man Boaz, that is, who belong to Christ, are the doctors and preachers. Ruth, humble and devout, signifies the devout and simple person who, by listening to sermons attentively, can derive things from them to inform her life and conscience.[75]

In the eighteenth century John Wesley commented on Naomi's question to Ruth in chapter 2:19, "'*Where hast thou gleaned today?*' It is a good question to ask ourselves in the evening, "Where have I gleaned today?" What improvements have I made in grace or knowledge? What have I learned or done, which will turn to account?'[76] A quotation from a contemporary commentator will demonstrate a completely different approach to interpreting the book of Ruth:

> Ruth is a story close to the realities of life in a peasant society with a subsistence economy ... Naomi and Ruth are both widows, while Ruth is also a resident alien. They belong to the classic categories of people who are needy because they lack economic security. The story tells how they acquire it. Ruth is a story about women's solidarity and resourcefulness in securing their future against the odds.[77]

The community of the church that reads and interprets Scripture also has a *cross-cultural* dimension to it. As Scripture is read and interpreted in communities across the world, our local and often narrowly self-interested understandings can be challenged and enhanced. For example, although many people would maintain a critical stance towards some of its ideological presuppositions, the hermeneutical practice of the Latin American theologies of liberation has had a profound impact on evangelical Bible engagement. The 1974 Lausanne Covenant includes the words, 'All of us are shocked by the poverty of millions and disturbed by the injustices which cause it. Those of us who live in affluent circumstances accept our duty to develop a simple lifestyle in order to contribute more generously to both relief and evangelism.'[78] Commenting on this statement, Peruvian theologian Samuel Escobar writes:

> We find ourselves facing an overwhelming fact: the Bible says a great deal, very clearly and powerfully, about poverty and oppression. We are disobedient to the Lord if we do not listen to the force of his Word in relation to this theme … It is encouraging to see the new generations of evangelicals uniting their missionary vision with a willingness to take on the responsibilities and risks of ministry in a world characterised by poverty. Are we ready to hear the Word of God when it speaks to us of this reality? Or do we prefer a capitalist or elitist ideology to close our eyes to this teaching?[79]

The cross-cultural nature of the interpretive community embraces both women and men. It is encouraging to discover women's readings of Scripture casting genuine new light:

> Feminist biblical criticism is an important current in contemporary study of the Bible. Undeniably it has raised our consciousness about a series of questions which professional interpretation of the Bible (whether in the pulpit or in academic scholarship) has commonly ignored, mainly, as we can now see, because it was almost entirely done by male interpreters who unthinkingly read the texts within a masculine horizon of interests. Women … are not only asking new questions but also thereby enabling us to see whole new dimensions of the meaning of the texts.[80]

We should be aware, as we think about the positive value of reading Scripture in community, that the community itself may collude in reading Scripture with prejudice or with an agenda that is oppressive for another community. As we saw in the case of Beyers Naudé, apartheid reading of Scripture legitimized racism, and selective Bible reading makes possible the proclamation of a 'prosperity gospel' that is untrue to the witness of God's word.

The importance of reading and interpreting Scripture in community does not negate the importance of study and meditation on our own. Personal reflection on God's word is crucial for our growth as followers of Jesus – but 'personal' is not the same as 'individualistic' which implies a rejection of other understandings and insights.

The Bible should be interpreted as a whole

> Whether in reading Scripture or conversing around the kitchen table, an isolated sentence can only be misunderstood. The more sentences we have, the deeper the sense of narrative is embedded in our minds and imaginations, and the more understanding is available. Matthew is incomprehensible separated from Exodus and Isaiah. Romans is an enigma without Genesis and Deuteronomy. Revelation is a crossword puzzle without Ezekiel and the Psalms.[81]

So writes Eugene Peterson in his passionate plea for an approach to Scripture that takes seriously the belief that this collection of different texts makes up a coherent narrative with a beginning, middle and end. The Bible is a 'meta-narrative', God's story that gives meaning to each human story. This approach, often referred to as 'canonical' interpretation because it will seek to take into account the whole 'canon' of Scripture, ensures that we will not read texts in isolation or interpret a text with no reference to other passages that may shed a different light on them from their immediate context. For example, as we will see in chapter 5, a puzzling passage like 1 Timothy 2:12, in which Paul appears to be limiting the ways in which women can express their spiritual gifts, must be read alongside texts like Galatians 3:28 and Joel 2 quoted by Peter in Acts 2:17, 18.

Those churches that have a tradition of liturgical Bible readings seek to ensure that the lectionary enables congregations to listen to the whole story of the Old and New Testaments. In some countries the Bible Societies and other Bible agencies organize 'Bible marathons', when the whole of Scripture is read in a public place, often in different languages, over a period of a few days. It is a wise practice to monitor on a regular basis the extent to which the whole of Scripture is being read in our congregations.

> Many debates within the church have been seriously hampered because there are parts of the foundation text – a verse here, a chapter

there – which have been quietly omitted from the church's public life. There is simply no excuse for missing out verses, paragraphs or chapters, from the New Testament in particular. We dare not try to tame the Bible. It is our foundation charter; we are not at liberty to play fast and loose with it.[82]

In recent years several biblical scholars have helped us to grasp how the Bible works as a one coherent story by encouraging us to understand it as a drama. One model suggests six acts in this drama:[83]

- Act 1   Creation
- Act 2   The Fall
- Act 3   The story of Israel
- Act 4   The story of Jesus
- Act 5   The story of the church
- Act 6   New creation

We will explore this idea further in chapter 9 when we consider how Jesus engaged with the Scriptures (see p. 000).

The Bible should be interpreted contextually – as it was written

In a lecture delivered in 1998, Dr Christopher Wright suggested that we might consider hermeneutics through three interdependent contextual lenses or focuses: author-centred interpretation, text-centred interpretation and reader-centred interpretation. He linked these ideas helpfully to three images that make them easy to remember: a window, a painting or similar work of art, and a mirror.[84]

Author-centred interpretation asks us to explore any Bible text by looking through it as a *window* onto the world of the Bible writer. This perspective encourages us to ask questions such as, 'Do we know who the writer was and when he wrote?' 'What can we reconstruct about the writer's background – his story, his presuppositions?' 'To what extent can we perceive the author's intention in writing this text?' 'For what kind of audience was this text intended?' It is easy to ask these questions, far less easy always to find answers! It is important that we take seriously the work of biblical scholars who seek to help the church 'in its task of going ever deeper into the meaning of scripture and so being refreshed and energized for the tasks to which we are called in and for the world.'[85]

The second lens that Wright proposes is that of text-centred interpretation, when we consider a Bible text as a *work of art*. Just as a painter selects the subject of his or her painting, its size and scope, what medium and colours will be used, so the Bible writers and editors created and edited works of different kinds – poems, songs, proverbs, visions, parables, letters. Within each genre they used their artistic skills to provide maximum impact. Consider the sophisticated construction of Lamentations, for example, in which each of the first four poems is an acrostic, every line starting with a consecutive letter of the Hebrew alphabet, or in the case of the central poem, all three lines of each strophe. The closing poem (Lam. 5) is not an acrostic, but its twenty-two verses hint at this form. Or look at the way Mark begins and ends the central section of his Gospel with two stories about opened eyes (8:22–26; 10:46–52). In both cases a man's life is transformed because Jesus heals his physical blindness. And in both cases Mark's narrative points us beyond the immediate story, to consider the theme of these chapters, the blindness of heart displayed by Jesus' closest followers.

One of the weaknesses of the 'inductive method' of Bible study (that is, the approach that encourages people to observe the Bible text, interpret it and then 'apply' it) is that while it has taught us to ask helpful questions about the Bible text, it has often encouraged superficiality in the answers. We may identify the genre of a Bible text correctly, but we do not then adapt our approach according to the genre. For example, we do not usually develop ways of preaching on poetry in the Bible that are different from preaching on narrative. The outcome is often a very homogenous, flattened handling of Scripture.

The Bible should be interpreted contextually – as it is encountered

Reader-centred interpretation of Scripture means that we interact with the Bible as a *mirror*.

> What can be seen in a mirror depends on who is standing in front of it … this is saying that the meaning in the text is not something … fixed and final in the text – some sort of objective reality. The meaning of the text actually only arises, only happens, in the act of reading … This approach reflects the shift from a modernity paradigm of exegesis to a post-modernity paradigm.[86]

We suggested earlier in this chapter that there is no such thing as a 'neutral' reading of Scripture. Our understanding of what we read and hear will inevitably be coloured by all that we mean by our 'worldview'. When we read how Scripture has been understood by the Church Fathers, by the medieval church, the Reformers, the early missionary movement, Catholics in Latin America and by women, we realize that all of these have looked into the 'mirror' of Scripture and understood it with their own cultural assumptions and in response to their particular context.

A reader-centred approach to Scripture is both a source of great enrichment and a risk. Fresh light is constantly cast on Scripture as people from different cultures and with different life experiences bring their insights together with God's eternal word. This is how this age-old word speaks freshly in every generation and in every culture. The risk is always that reader-centred interpretation will not be held together in creative tension with author and text-centred approaches, or even with other readers' responses, and can therefore become entirely subjective.

The Bible should be interpreted contextually – as it is lived out

With this third aspect of contextualized reading of Scripture, we come to the litmus test of our work of interpretation. The integrity with which we interpret the Bible will develop in direct relation to our openness to *act* on what we discover God saying to us in his word. Eugene Peterson provides a helpful case study of the connection between our reading and interpreting of Scripture and our living of it.[87] At the age of thirty-five he took up the sport he had practised as a student: he started running again. But he didn't just run; he also *read* about running – every book and magazine that he could lay his hands on. One day he pulled a muscle and had to give up his sport for a few months. Two weeks into his enforced inactivity he noticed he'd also stopped reading about running and began to see parallels with his experience of engaging with the Bible. If he wasn't actually running, then reading *about* running became pointless. His reading had become 'participatory', deepening and correcting and affirming his experience of running. If we are not really interested in participating in the life to which God's word calls us, we are not going to be interested in reading (or hearing) and interpreting that word so as to understand and respond to it in our everyday living.

> The most important question we ask of this text is not, 'What does this mean?' but 'What can I obey?' A simple act of obedience will

> open up our lives to this text far more quickly than any number of
> Bible studies and dictionaries and concordances.[88]

We can see clearly see the relationship between interpreting Scripture and living it out in the testimonies of chapter 1. Nurat was unaware of hermeneutics but she heard words of Scripture that related directly to her life experience, put them into practice and discovered that they 'worked' (p. 2). David Bruce went through a more conscious hermeneutical process of reinterpreting for his own circumstances Paul's testimony of conversion from prejudice (p. 3). He also discovered that response to the word of God opened further doors of understanding.

I wonder whether unease about the sermon with which this chapter started relates to the way that allegorical interpretation of Scripture often lets us off the hook of obedience, in this case the call to unprejudiced love of neighbour that is so clearly the context for Jesus' story of the Good Samaritan (Luke 10:29). At the same time, I recognize that Jesus himself is the Good Samaritan par excellence – and that brings us on to our next hermeneutical principle.

The Bible should be interpreted christologically

Christopher Wright closes his article on interpreting the Bible today by pleading for a 'missional reading' of Scripture – that is, one that constantly asks, 'What is the purpose of God behind all this? How is the text fitting into God's … mission and purpose?'[89] The focus of the Bible's account of God's missional purpose is the person of Jesus. So as we engage with God's word we will be alert to how any biblical text feeds into the story of God's purposes and signals the centrality of Jesus in those purposes. As we interact with any text of Scripture, it's helpful to keep in mind that there are always three possible 'levels' of interpretation:

- Level 1: the overarching Bible story of the mission and purpose of God
- Level 2: the particular historical context of this passage
- Level 3: the personal, domestic, intimate story

For example, the book of Ruth takes place at a specific historical moment in the story of God's people, 'in the days when the judges ruled' (1:1). It is a deeply personal, intimate story about famine, displacement, widowhood, family relationships, community responses, complaint against God, human kindness and compassion, marriage and birth. Lastly, it is a beautifully crafted piece of the Bible's jigsaw panorama of God's sovereign purposes, his surprising missional intentions. As we meditate on the significance of Ruth's story for our lives today, it will be most fruitful to keep all three of these 'levels' in mind.

Scripture should be interpreted relationally

The Bible can be interpreted and communicated in such a way that it becomes a means of oppression of others, of domination, of the loveless exercise of power. This is the accusation of many post-modern critics who reject the Bible as a 'totalizing' text. In response, we need to be alert to the misuse of Scripture and determine to keep at the heart of all our hermeneutical practice the commandments that Jesus told us were the greatest. Most of the conflicts that Jesus had with the religious leaders of his day centred on their legalistic readings of Scripture, interpretations that reinforced their worldview and their theological prejudices, and which had no concern for pastoral issues. When the Sadducees told a story intended to make the idea of resurrection look ridiculous, and demanded that Jesus respond to it with his interpretation of Deuteronomy 25:5, 6, he refused to play their games. 'You are wrong, because you know neither the scriptures or the power of God' (Matt. 22:29). These men read Scripture with minds already made up. Even more significantly for our practice of hermeneutics, when the Pharisees immediately afterwards tried to trap Jesus with the question about the greatest commandment, Jesus replied, 'You shall love the Lord your God with all your heart, and with all your soul, and with all your mind … You shall love your neighbour as yourself. On these two commandments hang all the law and the prophets' (Matt. 22:37, 39, 40). Kevin Vanhoozer suggests that

> What Christianity gives to hermeneutics is the contrast between a 'hermeneutics of the cross' and a 'hermeneutics of glory'. Those who read according to the hermeneutics of glory revel in their own interpretive skills, impose their interpretive theories on texts, and eclipse the text's own meaning … According to the hermeneutics of humility, by contrast, we will only gain understanding – of God, texts, others and ourselves – if we are willing to put ourselves second and our interpretive theories to the test of the text.[90]

The different approaches to interpreting the Bible that we have explored in this chapter are not interchangeable options. They are intended to work *together* in creative tension so that as we engage with Scripture and meditate on its meaning for our lives as individuals and communities, we 'will be progressively transformed into the image of him who is the ultimate object of the biblical witness.'[91]

5

Offensive Word

This teaching is difficult; who can accept it?
— **John 6:60**

'The real battle for Christians today is not Armageddon, it is the battle for a sensible approach to that ancient library of books we call the Bible.'[92] So wrote a Scottish church leader in a national newspaper in response to reports of groups and individuals who travelled to Israel in the closing days of 1999. These people had read the book of Revelation, especially chapter 20, and believed that Jesus would return to judge the world and rescue them from it in the first moments of the year 2000. They intended to be ready on the Mount of Olives to witness the event.

We would surely all support the plea for 'a sensible approach' to engaging with Scripture. But what constitutes 'sensible'? The same article talks about the 'strange and unpleasant document' whose references to a thousand years are 'the most fateful of the contributions of the Book of Revelation to last week's outbreak of psychosis'. There is no attempt on the part of the author to struggle with what it means to engage with the book of Revelation as precisely that: God's *revealed* word. Nor is there any consideration of Revelation *on its own terms*, the contextual terms that we thought about in chapter 4. Surely 'sensible' reading is contextual reading! Compare how another pastor and biblical scholar writes about the same book of the Bible:

> Is there no vision that can open our eyes to the abundant life of redemption in which we are immersed by Christ's covenant? ... For me, and for many, St John's Revelation has done it ... That St John

was a pastor, and wrote his Apocalypse as a pastor is too little taken
into account by his interpreters.[93]

Richard Holloway's newspaper article throws up two important truths. Firstly,
the Bible includes material that we may experience as 'strange and unpleasant',
uncongenial, even offensive. Secondly, *we have a choice* about how we interact
with these difficult texts. We can write them off as 'strange and unpleasant'
and, by implication, irrelevant. Or, because we believe that all of Scripture is
God's revelation, we can work at what it means to interact 'sensibly' with these
Bible texts or entire books.

In chapter 2 Jesus' parable of the sower helped us to explore why
it is that we may *resist* God's word rather than receive it and experience
its transforming power. We may resist because *we do not want to change*.
We engage with the Bible to affirm the status quo, reading selectively
and with our minds already made up about its significance. This is the
way millennial cults tend to read Scripture to fit their agendas. But we
may also resist because we have been on the receiving end of legalistic,
'dominant theology' readings of Scripture. The misuse of Genesis 3:16
when Olaniyi Daramola's mother was in labour is one such example (see
page 18). We can easily understand that she would be likely to find this
text painful and even offensive every time she read or heard it again. It
is this second kind of difficulty with God's word that we explore in this
chapter. If there are parts of the Bible that we close off because we find
them 'strange and unpleasant' or because we have experienced them as
oppressive and legalistic, we run the risk of closing off important ways in
which God can speak to us and bring about change in us. The passages of
the Bible that trouble us the most may be the ones to which we need to be
particularly alert!

In the rest of this chapter we explore the discomfort arising out of three
biblical themes that are problematic for many people:

- war and genocide
- the Bible's understanding of women
- the issue of homosexuality.

What does God require of us as we consider these issues? What is a 'sensible
approach' to them? How can we be faithful to God's word and love our
neighbour as ourselves in relation to these questions? These don't claim to
be complete explorations of the issues, but perhaps they can suggest some

approaches that make for life-giving interaction both with Scripture and with our neighbours, rather than destructive dead ends. If these issues are hard-trodden paths for you, I hope you may be encouraged to rake up the soil and let God's word drop into more receptive ground.

It's possible of course that some readers have never had a troubled thought about any of the themes that we explore here. This may be because of that respect for God's word that we discussed in chapter 3, or because we have simply never questioned the commonly accepted understandings of these texts that form part of our social and religious context. For example, I have not myself met a non-Western Christian who has expressed difficulty with the Old Testament war narratives. However, a colleague tells me that when she visited Rwanda after the 1994 genocide, texts such as Deuteronomy 20:16–17 and Joshua 8:18–29 were the focus of much anguished discussion. People's particular Bible stumbling blocks will vary and may take us by surprise. I vividly recall a workshop in Nigeria during which a young leader wept as he described his 'hatred' of Romans 9–11. For a range of reasons, this was the most problematic text in the Bible for him. The few passages in the Bible that directly address the question of homosexuality are painful for many Christians, most of all for those who are themselves of homosexual orientation. Women in both Western and non-Western cultures struggle with what some Bible texts appear to say about their role and with the way these texts are used in their churches and homes.

If we pastor others or accompany them in their exploration of Scripture, we will almost certainly be drawn in to help with the questions people ask about 'offensive' Bible texts. Even if we ourselves have never found any Bible passage problematic, we can learn to respect the questions of others and be prepared to respond caringly and thoughtfully to those who genuinely find parts of the Bible difficult. Discussing Paul's complex arguments in Romans 3, Tom Wright comments:

> It is important to think things through. We may not always be able to understand God and his ways with the world. But we must not shirk the intellectual challenge that meets us at every point. If we are to love God with our minds as well as with heart, soul and strength (Mark 12:30) it is important to follow the arguments through as far as we can – while always having the humility to recognize that we may not be able to see round the corner into the innermost secrets.[94]

Before reading further, take time to identify any Bible passages that you have experienced as 'offensive', texts that cause you distress or raise questions for you, passages that you would prefer not to find in God's word. Try to explore what it is about them that causes these reactions. If you have never had any struggles with parts of the Bible, try to identify why this is the case.

War in Scripture

Towards the end of his life my father, who loved God's word and had worked for many years as a Bible translator in Peru, began hesitantly to express the distress he was experiencing as he re-read some Old Testament texts. The passages that raised the most disturbing questions for him were the war narratives that speak of a God who appears to ordain genocide, the stories that have caused some Rwandan Christians much anguish. My father's questions prompted me to go back and explore a theme that I had not thought about much in the twenty years or so since I first discussed it with South African friends. These were Christians who paid the price for taking a pacifist stance in their country during the civil conflicts of the late 1980s. The book I found most helpful was Peter Craigie's *The Problem of War in the Old Testament*.[95]

Reflecting on the Bible's narratives about war, Craigie urges us to be aware of our reactions to them. Are we disturbed by the ruthlessness of the rules of engagement laid out in Deuteronomy 20:10–18 or the pitiless warfare of Joshua and Judges? If not, maybe we should be! Or do we somehow 'manage' these war narratives so that they do not trouble us? Do we spiritualize or allegorize them, interpreting, for example, the story of the capture of Jericho in Joshua 6 as a picture of the spiritual triumph of people who obey God whole-heartedly? Craigie does not condemn such interpretations but insists that we must understand that the biblical writers were describing the actual killing of human beings – non-combatant civilians – and that 'a similar event in Vietnam was followed by a war crimes trial.'[96] Another common response to these texts is a tendency to be generally negative about the Old Testament and to prefer to engage (for example in a Bible discussion group) only with the New Testament or the less problematic texts of the Old. For Arab Christians today, the biblical accounts of wars of occupation are deeply problematic. A colleague who has spent time with Syrian and Lebanese Christians reports that they simply do not read much of the Old Testament. We may also resort to a 'two Gods' understanding of the Bible: the judgmental warrior God of the Old Testament, and the New Testament's loving and merciful God of grace revealed in Jesus. More liberal readers of the Old Testament tend to write off the stories of war and slaughter simply as history written by the conquerors.

We can helpfully break down the questions that arise from reading books like Deuteronomy, Joshua and Judges into three categories:

- questions about the identity of God
- questions about why the Bible contains so much material about war and violence and how we can understand this as 'revelation'
- questions about the relevance of these narratives for guiding our behaviour as Christians.

Can God 'the warrior' (Exod. 15:3) who directs his people to annihilate the nations of Canaan, leaving nothing that breathes to remain alive (Deut. 20:16–17) be the unchanging God of love revealed in Jesus (Mal. 3:6; John 14:9; 1 John 4:8)? The warrior identity of God is not a biblical sideline but a major theme in all but three of the books of the Old Testament (Ruth, the Song of Songs and Esther – though some of the behaviour of Esther and her allies raises the same issues – see Esther 8:7–13). The title 'Lord of Hosts' means 'Lord of the Armies' and is found over two hundred times in the Old Testament. Nor does the New Testament negate the understanding of a warrior God who battles for his people: Paul and Stephen both refer positively to the Exodus (Acts 7:35–36; 13:17), 'the event which marked the inauguration of the conception of God as Warrior in ancient Israel.'[97] The biblical revelation of God as a warrior is nevertheless a *partial* revelation; it is by no means the full story of God's identity revealed in his word, even in the Old Testament. His people also experienced him there as the tender Father (Hos. 11:3–4; Isa. 63:15–16), the caring Shepherd (Ezek. 34:11–16) and the compassionate Husband (Isa. 54:5–8).

Craigie proposes several helpful directions for reflecting on these issues. Firstly, the narratives of the Old Testament tell us about a God who chooses to reveal himself through his *participation in ordinary, sinful, human history*, especially in relation to his people Israel: 'the form which the Kingdom of God assumed in Old Testament times was that of a *nation state*, the state of God's chosen people.'[98] The nation of Israel was born out of the normal political struggle of an oppressed people, the kind of struggle that has characterized the independence conflicts of America or India with

Britain, of African nations with their various colonists, or the Latin American peoples with Spain and Portugal. After the initial liberation of the people of Israel from Egypt, in which God's activity is characterized in the book of Exodus as miraculous, the story follows the normal human pattern of a people fighting for land and identity against hostile competitors, a people *necessarily* engaging in the evil of war, and, later in their history, civil war (2 Sam. 13, for example).[99] The Bible portrays war realistically, as 'an act of violence intended to compel our opponent to fulfil our will'.[100] Unlike much of today's euphemistic communication about war, Scripture is unflinchingly realistic about its horrors. It does not speak the language of 'collateral damage' or 'extraordinary rendition', those weasel words that seek to disguise the destruction and suffering that war inevitably produces; the prophets often recoil with horror at the realities of war (Ezek. 7:14–27, Nah. 2:1–13). The Old Testament bears witness, not to a superhuman people of God, protected from ugly realities, but to a small and vulnerable nation in formation through ordinary political processes that inevitably include war:

> God determined, in some sense, the outcome of human events by participating through the *normal* forms of human activity; God, as Warrior, fought *through* the fighting of his people … If the precondition for experiencing the presence of God in human, historical existence were that the persons and activities concerned must be sinless … God's presence in history would never be known at all … God's presence in such a situation (war, for example) will not justify it or make it holy, but it does provide hope in a situation of hopelessness.[101]

Secondly, God participates in human history in order to bring about both *judgment* and *salvation*. This understanding demands that we take a long view of biblical history, that we engage with *all* of the Old Testament, not only the accounts of Israel's conquests but also her defeats. We consider first the question of judgment. The annihilation that God ordained for the peoples of Canaan *should* disturb us, as indeed the Bible's teaching on God's judgment should always disturb us. As we reflect on what happened to the peoples of Canaan, we find ourselves asking, with Abraham, 'Will you indeed sweep away the righteous with the wicked? … Shall not the Judge of all the earth do what is just?' (Gen. 18:23, 25). We hear the Lord's warning to his people through Moses as they stand on the edge of the Jordan: 'Do not say to yourself, "It is because of my righteousness that the Lord has brought me in to occupy this land"; it is rather because of the wickedness of these nations that the Lord is dispossessing them before you' (Deut. 9:4). As we ask questions about the identity of God revealed in Scripture, we must take into account that he is also known as the one who 'hates the lover of violence' (Ps. 11:5) and, above all, as the God whose final judgment of the peoples will bring about unimaginable peace, transform swords into ploughshares and bring an end to all war (Isa. 2:2–4). We must hold in faithful tension the accounts of apparently wholesale destruction with, for example, God's mercy on Lot and his family in Sodom (Gen. 19:15–16, 29) and the safekeeping of Rahab in Jericho (Josh. 6:17). The Old Testament bears witness to the God who takes no pleasure in the death of wicked people, but longs that they 'should turn from their ways and live' (Ezek. 18:21–23). We are called to remain faithful to a biblical record in which:

> God is presented … as employing the (politically unavoidable) wars of the Hebrew conquest as a means of divine judgment on evil nations, just as later he was to employ the victorious warfare of foreign nations in the execution of his judgment upon his own chosen people.[102]

Such faithful reading is important today, in a world racked by war and civil conflict. During the Falklands / Malvinas war of 1982, Dr René Padilla preached on the theme of war in his church in Buenos Aires. His sermons on Habakkuk drew courageous and uncomfortable parallels between contemporary events and the actions of God in judging his own people and the surrounding nations:

> I cannot get away from the thought that the God who acted in grace and judgment in the Old Testament is the same God who continues to act in grace and judgment today … I do believe that Argentina has been under the judgment of God. There has been a lot of corruption and exploitation of the poor and now God is acting.

But the war was also to be understood as a warning to Britain, the 'victor' in the conflict. Padilla pointed out that: 'Judgment will also come to the empire'; the Bible records that those nations that God allowed to be instruments of judgment on Israel in due course came under God's judgment themselves for their wrongdoing and injustice – the Assyrians at the hands of the Babylonians and the Babylonians of the Persians.[103]

We move now to the theme of salvation. The Old Testament story of God's saving purposes is paradoxically linked to the theme of his people's *defeats* rather than to their successes in battle. The nation state of Israel failed under the terms of the original covenant to be the people of God whose goodness and integrity would demonstrate to the surrounding nations the true identity of the Lord (Deut. 4:5–8). It is out of the desolate stories of God's judgment on his people in their defeats in wars with Egypt, Assyria, Babylon and Persia that is born the hope of something entirely new, a more profound understanding both of humanity's failure and of the identity of God and his purposes. The prophets begin to speak of a new covenant that has no external political form. 'It will not be like the covenant that I made with their ancestors … a covenant that they broke … But this is the covenant that I will make … I will put my law within them … on their hearts; and I will be their God, and they shall be my people' (Jer. 31:32–33). It is out of the defeat and exile of God's people and the failure of their political institutions that there comes the promise of the paradoxical Saviour King, 'triumphant and victorious … humble and riding on a donkey' (Zech. 9:9).[104]

Down the centuries people of all kinds, including Christians, have neglected the significance of the Old Testament narratives of defeat and misused the stories of conquest and slaughter for their own ends. Augustine and Calvin are among those who interpreted certain Bible texts to justify the destruction of people identified as heretics or enemies of God and to engage in so-called 'holy wars', the Crusades being the worst example.[105] In recent times, carefully selected quotations from the Bible have been included in US presidential briefings about the Iraq war.[106] It is easy to point the finger at such examples. The truth is that we *all* have a tendency to resist the uncongenial biblical theme of weakness, and the evidence that it is so often God's mysterious way of bringing about his purposes. We need to return often to walk the Emmaus road, to recognize our own foolishly selective reading of God's word and to let Jesus remind us that the witness of 'all the scriptures', of 'all that the prophets have declared' is that the way to glory leads through suffering, weakness and apparent defeat (Luke 24:25–27).

Women in Scripture

A few years ago a friend was telling me about his sabbatical in the USA. One Sunday morning he was in church – in Boston, if I remember rightly. One of the lectionary readings that morning was from Paul's first letter to Timothy: 'Let a woman learn in silence with full submission. I permit no woman to teach or to have authority … For … the woman was deceived … Yet she will be saved through childbearing' (1 Tim. 2:11–15). As the reading ended, the congregation started to boo angrily. This was a very 'offensive' word for them.

I wonder how you respond to this anecdote. With shock, or perhaps sadness, that people – especially people in church – reacted to God's word like this? Or more hopefully? At least they were *listening* to the reading! Or do you perhaps remember times when you have read or heard this text or other similar ones, and felt inner turmoil that you would never dream of expressing publicly? I'm not taking it for granted that it is only women readers of this book who may find Paul's directions to Timothy 'offensive'. There are many Christian men for whom this text presents difficulties, as indeed there are plenty of women and men for whom it presents no problem! Examining our reactions to Bible texts that are problematic for one group of people or another can be instructive. It develops our understanding of those factors in our personal context that influence how we interpret and understand Scripture. You might like to look back at the practical exercise that was suggested in chapter 4, pages 48–49.

The texts in the Bible that may be problematic for us because of the way they talk about women fall into two main categories. Firstly there are those passages like 1 Timothy 2:8–15 and 1 Corinthians 11:2–16 that relate to women's role in church and society. Secondly, there are the Old Testament narratives that portray women as victims of the careless, even violent, behaviour of men and therefore – as some commentators suggest – somehow legitimize violence towards women. Once again, we cannot explore these issues fully here. I simply aim to suggest what may be helpful directions and emphases.

Two of the hermeneutical principles that we unpacked in chapter 4 were, firstly, the requirement to read Scripture *as a whole*, 'allowing Scripture to interpret Scripture, and seeking to understand the broad sweep of God's dealings with humanity, from creation to new creation.' Secondly, there is the requirement to try to read *contextually, as Scripture was written*, 'acknowledging the Bible's different literary forms and seeking to understand the author's intention and the historical and canonical context of a passage.'[107] We have already seen these principles at work in the previous section on war. That uncongenial theme demands a long view of biblical history, a recognition of the significance of the narratives of *defeat* alongside the narratives of *conquest*. A hermeneutically principled approach involves acknowledging the evidence of God's acts of mercy alongside the accounts of judgment; it involves asking questions about the intentions of the human authors of these narratives alongside the affirmation of our faith in these texts as God's revelation. We must do this same kind of work when we examine what the Bible has to say about women, and we must seek to do so with integrity:

> If our interpretation is not to be subject to immovable prejudice, we must attend to the particularity of the texts and the persons and situations they portray and be open to the perhaps surprising possibilities they disclose ... Blinkered use of a feminist hermeneutic of suspicion is much like an old-fashioned form of dogmatic theological interpretation, which knew in advance what was to be found in all the texts and whose exegesis of them was just one illustration after another of predetermined dogmas.[108]

The text we must start with in exploring this issue is Genesis 1:26–31, the first account of creation. It underpins the rest of the story of men and women in the Bible. Here God reveals his intention to 'make humankind in our image, according to our likeness ... So God created humankind in his image ... male and female he created them' (Gen. 1:26–27; 5:1–2). This account makes it clear that in God's good creation, in a world not yet distorted by sin, man and woman *equally* reflected the image of God, with all the mysterious depths that implies, and *equally* exercised responsibility before their Creator over the creation (Gen. 1:28–30).

The second creation narrative in Genesis 2:4b-25 presents us with different material. God creates the man first (2:7) and places him in the garden where, as well as the trees provided for food, there grow the 'tree of life' and the 'tree of the knowledge of good and evil' (2:8–9). God commissions the man to care for Eden and carefully warns him about the single tree whose fruit he is not to eat (2:15–17). In all the beauty of his creation God now finds only one thing 'not good' – that the man he has created is alone (2:18). Birds and animals, for all their beauty and variety, cannot provide the companionship and intimacy that God has in mind if human beings are truly to reflect the relational nature of his image: 'for the man there was not found a helper as his partner' (2:20). Only with the woman that God now creates does the man at last experience completeness (2:23–25). Genesis 3 then narrates the unravelling of this scene of harmony, the events that culminate in the catastrophe of the fall. The serpent presents the woman with a powerfully seductive alternative version of the truth about life in God's world. Apparently with little struggle she succumbs to this false vision, and invites her husband to participate also in the act of rebellious autonomy that destroys all harmony with their creator (3:1–7).

Genesis 2 and 3 have often been interpreted as implying that woman is inherently subordinate and inferior to man because God created her only after creating man and only as his helper. Worse still, she was instrumental in bringing about the catastrophe of the fall. Paul's reference to Genesis 2 and 3 in 1 Timothy 2:13–14 might seem to support this understanding. But the principles of interpreting Scripture surely make it impossible to come to this conclusion with any integrity. For a start, the Hebrew word translated variously in Genesis 2:18 as 'helper', 'companion' or 'partner' is *ezer*. In the rest of the Old Testament this word usually describes God himself, as in Exodus 18:4, 'The God of my father was my *help*, and delivered me from the sword of Pharaoh', or Psalm 70:5, 'You are my *help* and my deliverer; O Lord, do not delay!' There is nothing second-rate about this helper! If woman is inferior to man because she was created after him, then logically, man is inferior to the animals because he was created after them! In addition, as we bear in mind the hermeneutical requirement to 'allow Scripture to interpret Scripture' and 'to bring our understanding of Scripture back to Scripture'[109] we see that this understanding of 1 Timothy 2:11–15 is simply incompatible with so much else that Paul writes in his letters. Consider his great affirmation in Galatians 3:26, 28 that, 'in Christ Jesus you are all children of God through faith … there is no longer male and female; for all of you are one in Christ Jesus.' Reflect on how Paul affirmed and valued women in the early church: women such as Prisca, the teacher – alongside her husband – of Apollos (Rom. 16:3 and Acts 18:24–26); Phoebe, a deacon or minister in the church at Cenchreae (Rom. 16:1); and Junia, 'prominent among the apostles' (Rom. 16:7).[110] Paul was no misogynist! He did not hate women.

We therefore need to read Paul's words in 1 Timothy with great care and open minds to try to understand what implications he really is drawing from Genesis 2 and 3.

Elsewhere Paul makes clear that he *expects* women to be involved in public prayer and proclamation of God's word (1 Cor. 11:5, 13). This accords with Peter's sermon on the day of Pentecost and Joel's vision of the universal work of God's Spirit (Acts 2:17–18). It is difficult for us to grasp the subversive and revolutionary nature of Paul's injunction to women to 'learn' (1 Tim. 2:11). For him, the story of Adam and Eve is an example of what can happen when women have *not* had the opportunity to learn. Writing to his young disciple Timothy, Paul is surely insisting that women need to be able to pray and prophesy *with the advantages of learning* that in his day were normally the prerogative of men. The Genesis 2 narrative tells us that Adam was created first and received direct instructions from God about the tree of the knowledge of good and evil (2:16–17); Eve, created later, received this instruction second hand from her husband. He is then described as being 'with her' as she takes the fruit and eats (3:6). It is difficult to read the Genesis narrative of creation and fall and come to Paul's conclusion that 'Adam was not deceived', unless he means that Adam was not deceived directly by the serpent (1 Tim. 2:14) or that he knew what he was doing when he took the fruit from Eve's hand. Elsewhere Paul writes only of 'the transgression of Adam' and of 'one man's disobedience' (Rom. 5:14, 19). The implication of this is surely that all opportunities for theological reflection and exploring the Christian faith must be available to women and men alike so that *both* may equally serve the purposes of God's kingdom in communicating his truth in action and word.

What then about the puzzle of 1 Timothy 2:15, one of the most problematic texts in Scripture? In the light of Paul's other teaching, childbearing cannot be understood as a *condition* of salvation (Rom. 3:23–24; Eph. 2:8). What hope would there be for childless or single women? The Greek verb *sozo* that Paul uses here means both 'to save' or 'to keep safe', in the sense of spiritual salvation (as in 1 Tim. 2:4) and of physical safety or rescue (as in Matt. 8:25). Different English Bible translations reveal different theologies:

- 'Yet she will be saved through childbearing' (NRSV)
- 'Nevertheless she will be saved in childbearing' (NKJV)
- 'But women will be saved by having children' (CEV)
- 'On the other hand, her childbearing brought about salvation' (*The Message*)
- 'Nevertheless I believe that women will come safely through childbirth' (J. B. Phillips)
- 'Nevertheless [the sentence put upon women of pain in motherhood does not hinder their souls' salvation, and] they will be saved [eternally]' (Amplified Bible)
- Several translations, such as the GNB, put the translation 'will be kept safe through childbirth' in a footnote.

As we consider these different understandings, we will need to reflect together with our Christian community on the extent to which we have been conditioned by our church tradition and cultural context to understand this text in a certain way. Maybe the time has come to reconsider our interpretations. If so, how might this affect our attitudes to women, and especially single women or those who do not have children?

We are not yet finished with some foundational thinking about men and women in Genesis. Paul's words on childbirth bring us to our next interpretational challenge. How are we to understand God's words addressed to Eve, recorded in Genesis 3:16: 'I will greatly increase your pangs in childbearing; in pain you shall bring forth children, yet your desire shall be for your husband, and he shall rule over you'? A few years ago, at a meeting in Moscow on Christian responses to HIV/AIDS in Russia and other former Soviet countries, a group of us spent time exploring biblical teaching that might help us to develop ways of working with young people to reduce the incidence of the disease. Experience in Africa has clearly shown that merely to urge young people to practise sexual abstinence or make 'right choices' is not adequate or realistic. Many women in Africa and elsewhere have *no* choice when faced by men who demand sex. The impact of the fall described by God in Genesis 3:16 precisely describes the kind of relationship between the sexes in which AIDS thrives. The mutuality and equality between man and woman that characterized their relationship before the fall has now become distorted into domination on the part of the man and in the woman an unreciprocated, often manipulative, yearning for unity and intimacy.

It is not only within marriage that we encounter the distortions of the fall in relationships between men and women. They can be seen whenever women and men, single, married and widowed, relate in unhealthy ways. At the Moscow meeting we discussed whether in Genesis 3:16 God is sadly describing to Adam and Eve the catastrophic disorder resulting from what they had done, or ordaining how things *should* be from now on? I was shaken to discover that a number of the group understood the words to describe how things *should* be, because God had ordained it so. We have already seen the outcome of this kind of thinking in the case of my Nigerian friend's mother, forced by her church leaders to endure an appallingly long and painful labour (p. 18). But *is* this how we are to understand God's words? The German theologian Helmut Thielicke, among many others, did not believe so. He wrote that the domination of woman by man is 'not an imperative order of creation, but rather the element of disorder that disturbs the original peace.'[111]

The Old Testament presents us with many examples of how this profound disorder played out in the history of God's people. The stories of Lot's willingness to hand over his daughters to the men bent on homosexual rape (Gen. 19:4–8), Amnon's incestuous violation of Tamar (2 Sam. 13:1–22), the sacrifice of Jephthah's daughter (Judg. 11:29–40) and the grim account of the gang rape of an anonymous woman (Judg. 19:1–30) all bear witness to how seriously sin distorted God's intention for the relationship between men and women. Beyond these 'texts of terror' are many more stories in the Old Testament of men's careless treatment of women and of women's manipulative dependence on men. Abraham's treatment of Hagar (Gen. 16:1–16; 21:9–21) and David's adultery with Bathsheba and murder of her husband (2 Sam. 11) would be two such examples. These accounts raise the same questions for us as the war narratives of the Old Testament. Why are they included as part of the story through which God reveals himself? We said of the war narratives that they tell us of a God who participates in ordinary, sinful, human history. These terrible stories of distorted relationships between men and women are part of the same sinful narrative; they tell us what happens when human beings, even among God's chosen people, even among his chosen leaders, abandon his ways. They are never given to us as examples to imitate. Narratives such as the book of Ruth reveal the possibilities, even in the Old Testament, of redeemed relationships between women and men. Boaz is a rare case of an Old Testament male who is counter-cultural in relation to the women in his life. (However, when women discuss this story in some parts of Africa, the 'hermeneutic of suspicion' that arises out of their common experience often identifies Boaz as an older man out to get a young wife.)

Astonishingly, these Bible stories of violence can be life-giving and deeply relevant in many contexts around the world today. For example, the Ujamaa Centre for Biblical and Theological Community Development and Research in South Africa launched the 'Tamar Campaign' in 2000. A friend told me about a Bible study he attended in Mozambique. In it, Ujamaa's Maria Makgamathe led an interactive discussion on the rape of Tamar in 2 Samuel 13:1–24 that exposed contemporary attitudes towards rape in African society:

> The men were able to see how our attitudes often parallel those of many of the male characters in this biblical narrative – Amnon, Jonadab, Absalom, David – who in various ways contributed to Tamar's rape and its tragic aftermath. Tamar's resistance and lament were prophetic cries that visibly empowered the women gathered there at the conference.[112]

I suggest that this kind of experiential exploration of these violent texts is every bit as relevant in Western contexts where the incidence of rape and abuse continues to rise.

The testimony of the four Gospels is that Jesus himself is the most powerful example of the truth that the domination of women by men and the unhealthy dependence on men by women are not imperative orders of creation. Jesus bore witness constantly to the possibility of redeemed relationships. As a single man, he sought out and appreciated the company of women like Mary and Martha of Bethany (John 11:5), the woman at the Samaria well (John 4) and those who were on his mission team – Mary Magdalene, Joanna, Susanna 'and many others' as Luke records (Luke 8:1–3). Jesus welcomed the physical touch of women but never exploited it (Matt. 9:20–22; Luke 7:36–50). He encouraged Mary of Bethany to cross the boundary into the place of a disciple normally occupied by men (Luke 10:38–42). And it was to a woman – Mary Magdalene – that Jesus first revealed himself after the resurrection (John 20:11–18). For the male leaders of Jesus' disciples, the witness of Mary and the other women to the resurrection seemed 'an idle tale, and they did not believe them' (Luke 24: 11). Their thinking was shaped by prevailing social attitudes to the testimony of women, one of the groups whose 'voices from the margins' are so important today in enriching our understanding of the power of Scripture to speak to us.[113]

Homosexuality in Scripture

Among my papers is an anonymous letter that I treasure. It came in response to a comment I once wrote in one of Scripture Union's Bible guides. Reflecting on the uncaring legalism of the Pharisees in Mark 10:1–12, I suggested that Christian churches must always seek to be communities characterized by the kind of acceptance and understanding that Jesus models for us in the Gospels. This acceptance must be unconditional, whether people's marriages are failing or they are struggling with the homosexual or lesbian person's longing to 'become one flesh' (Mark 10:8). This is part of the letter:

> We are a group of Christians who moved to be part of a ministry to the sexually broken. For most of us, that meant how to live as a Christian with a homosexual orientation. God has been very good to me over the last fifteen years, although life has been hard. From time to time I receive encouragement that I am not alone. You touched my heart when you wrote about churches where 'we seek to understand the unique loneliness of homosexual orientation'. I was so surprised to read that in a Christian publication that I had to re-read it several times … an indication of how starved I am to hear things like that from a Christian. Know that you gave water to a parched soul. I look forward to meeting you in heaven.

I realize that for some readers it may be inconceivable that anyone might be both Christian and of homosexual orientation, as this man is. Hopefully his letter may at least encourage you to be open to this possibility. We will return later to the issue of the 'unique loneliness' of homosexual people.

In reading some of what Christians of different persuasions and cultures have written in recent years on this issue, I've found both widespread acknowledgment of the complexities and encouraging humility. For example, American theologian Marva Dawn writes of her hesitations in tackling the subject:

> The debates about homosexual behaviour threaten to divide many church bodies and alienate many people on both sides of the issue. Especially distressing is the violence manifested both by those who believe that homosexual behaviour should be accepted by the Church and by those who claim that the Bible forbids such activity … we recognize … that such violence and hostility are contrary to the virtues of the Kingdom of God. Therefore, we want to enter into the debates about homosexuality with the utmost patience and gentleness and love.[114]

Mennonite scholar Mark Thiessen Nation reminds us of the reasons for the 'strong rhetoric' that marks the debates about homosexuality. Fear of 'rigidly defined orthodoxy' on one side and anxiety on the other about 'moral and theological confusion and spiritual sickness' in the church come together with the fact that

> this is not just an 'issue' but is connected to people. We are talking about family, friends and brothers and sisters in Christ – in short, relationships. If anyone fails to understand why parents of gay or lesbian children, even parents who are theologically very conservative, come to have strong feelings about this issue, then they have a failure of imagination – or compassion.[115]

Paul's discussion in Romans 1:18–27 probably constitutes the most 'offensive' text in the Bible for people of homosexual orientation. His argument seems to focus on homosexuality as the *paradigm* of what has gone wrong with the world. His reference to creation and to God's original intention of 'natural intercourse' (vs. 26, 27) is deeply painful for the many men and women for whom same-sex attraction has been lifelong, a core aspect of their identity. It is also painful for those whose homosexuality originates in abuse as a vulnerable young person who might otherwise have developed as a heterosexual. Marva Dawn helpfully draws on Richard B. Hays' thinking to insist on the need to separate the tasks of exegesis and hermeneutics in examining this text in Romans. That is, we have to do good work on exploring what the text *actually says* ('reading contextually as it was written') before we seek to discern how we may understand it for our lives ('reading contextually as it is encountered and lived out today'). Romans 1:26, 27 appears within the context of Paul's developing argument in this chapter about how the gospel reveals God's righteousness – his justice and integrity (Rom. 1:17) – as opposed to the unrighteousness of 'those who by their wickedness suppress the truth' (v. 18):

> All depravities follow from the radical rebellion of human beings against their Creator. Hays concludes that 'the passage is not merely a polemic denunciation of selected pagan vices; it is a diagnosis of the human condition.'[116]

Tom Wright shares this approach in his commentary on the same text in Romans:

> [Paul] is talking about the human race as a whole. His point is not 'there are some exceptionally wicked people out there who do these revolting things' but 'the fact that such clear distortions of the creator's male-plus-female intention occur in the world indicates that the human race as a whole is guilty of a character-twisting idolatry' … we find here and elsewhere in the New Testament, not a set of arbitrary rules, but a deep theology of what it means to be genuinely human, and a warning about the apparently infinite capacity of human beings for self-deception.[117]

The ticking bomb that Paul plants in the first verses of Romans 2 bears out this understanding: 'Therefore you have no excuse, whoever you are, when you judge others; for in passing judgement on another you condemn yourself … Do you imagine, whoever you are, that when you judge those who do such things and yet do them yourself, you will escape the judgement of God?' To read on into Romans 2 is to read *contextually* and responsibly what Paul has to say about homosexual behaviour; to draw conclusions from chapter 1 without taking chapter 2 into account is quite simply prejudiced Bible engagement.

Nowhere in Scripture do we find justification for condemning homosexual behaviour as worse than any other sin. 1 Corinthians 6:9, 10 lists homosexual behaviour, including homosexual prostitution, alongside thieving, greed, drunkenness, adultery and heterosexual promiscuity. The Corinthian church embraced people in *all* these categories because *all* had been 'washed … sanctified … justified' (v.11). 1 Timothy 1:9, 10 similarly lists homosexual behaviour alongside slave-traders, liars and perjurers. Richard Hays believes that the expression 'against nature' (Rom. 1:26) 'probably did not carry for Paul and his readers the vehement connotation of "monstrous abomination" which it subsequently acquired in Western thought about homosexuality. Consequently this phrase should certainly not be adduced as if it were a biblical warrant for the frantic homophobia which sometimes prevails in modern society.'[118]

Hays is talking about a Western context, but what about this issue in the non-Western world? Attitudes to homosexuality vary greatly in the world's different cultures. In 2007 a survey by the Pew Foundation found that:

> People in Africa and the Middle East strongly object to societal acceptance of homosexuality. But there is far greater tolerance for homosexuality in major Latin American countries such as Mexico, Argentina, Chile and Brazil. Opinion in Europe is split between West and East. Majorities in every Western European nation surveyed say homosexuality should be accepted by society, while most Russians, Poles and Ukrainians disagree. Americans are divided – a thin plurality (49%) believes homosexuality should be accepted, while 41% disagree.[119]

In the light of these contextual differences in attitudes, it is all the more important for Christians to be alert to how our cultures shape the way that we read what Scripture says both about homosexuality and about how we are called to relate to those people of homosexual orientation who are so often marginalized and despised. In all African countries, with the exception of South Africa, it is virtually impossible for any Christian to admit a homosexual orientation without being ostracized or worse. It also takes great courage for any Christian publicly to befriend someone of homosexual orientation. Under the Sharia law of Muslim culture, people of homosexual orientation may be stoned to death or hanged, as in the case of two teenagers in Iran in 2005.

I want to close this chapter by reflecting again on how selectively we read Scripture. We recognize instinctively that when God says, 'It is not good that the man should be alone' (Gen. 2:18) he is affirming an essential aspect of what it means to be human. Human beings are made to be in relationship, reflecting the relational character of the Trinity. But when it comes to people of homosexual orientation, we often deny their need to live in relationship, or rather, we are unrealistic about what is involved in such relationship. Many Christians, reflecting on this issue, come to the same conclusion as Marva Dawn:

> When I ask homosexuals for celibacy, I am not asking anything more of them than I asked of myself all the years that I was single. Celibacy was a good (but sometimes painfully difficult) choice for me in order to be faithful to the purposes of God.[120]

I believe this to be an understandable, but inadequate response. With rare exceptions, Christian men and women of homosexual orientation who seek to be faithful to Scripture have to endure a 'unique loneliness', unlike the loneliness of heterosexual celibacy. They cannot risk getting close to another person of either gender without disclosing the truth of their condition. Disclosure often leads to rejection or worse. For men and women of both homosexual and heterosexual orientation, loneliness (which is different from solitude) is the greatest threat to good celibacy, the kind of single life that Jesus lived out.[121] It was when he was alone in the desert that Jesus experienced the greatest pressures of temptation and the devil's insistent questions about his identity (Luke 4:3, 9). We cannot demand that people of homosexual orientation live lives of righteousness, reflecting the beauty and order of God's truth that Paul outlines in Romans 1:17 if we are not prepared to offer them embrace rather than exclusion. I write this with a heavy heart, recognizing my own failure in rejecting a woman friend who kept the reality of her sexual orientation from me for several years. When she finally summoned the courage to tell me the truth, it was only to experience my rejection. I'm astonished and humbled that she still considers me a friend.

Rejection and loneliness can take a terrible toll. A few years ago a young African Christian leader known to friends of mine took his own life. Since childhood he had struggled with his homosexual orientation. He had been open about it, sought professional Christian help, asked God for change that never came. The note that he left for his friends and family ended with these words: 'I am so looking forward to heaven, where there is neither marriage nor giving in marriage.'

In our hermeneutical practice, and especially as we engage with the 'offensive word', we urgently need God's grace to fulfil his requirement to 'do justice, and to love kindness, and to walk humbly' with him and with our brothers and sisters in Christ (Mic. 6:8).

6

Unique Word

Lord, to whom can we go?
You have the words of eternal life

— John 6:68

In an absorbing and moving account of his search for assurance of salvation, Sultan Muhammed Paul, an aristocratic Afghani, describes his careful examination of the scriptures of his own faith: 'What I found out through studying the Qur'an was what I had known before: attaining salvation is dependent upon doing good works.' Disturbed by the Qur'an's references to universal human sinfulness and a deep sense of his own unworthiness of salvation, this man then found himself considering the Qur'an's account of the sinlessness of the Prophet Jesus. Comparing it with the testimony of the *Injil*, the Christian Gospels, he found that their evidence concurred with the Qur'an: 'There is solid evidence to prove that, with the exception of the Prophet Jesus, all mankind are sinful … who was I that I should claim to be able to gain salvation by good works, when many religious leaders, philosophers and saints had failed to run this impossible course?' Research now turned to desperate prayer as this man cast himself on God's mercy: 'O God, my Creator and my Lord … You know how long I have been seeking Your true religion. I have carried my investigation as far as I have been able. Now, therefore, open to me the door of Your knowledge and Your salvation.' Opening the *Injil* once again, he found his eyes focused on words in Matthew's Gospel, 'Come to me, all you that are weary and are carrying heavy burdens and I will give you rest' (11:28). 'For a sinner like me, it was indeed the supreme proclamation of good news … The Messiah claims: "I will give you rest." He shows how salvation depends upon Him. He does not merely point to a path which is above or beyond Him, but says: "I am the way, and the truth, and the life. No one comes to the Father except through Me" (John 14:6).'[122]

The evidence recorded here of the interplay between the Muslim and Christian Scriptures, the Holy Spirit and the seeking human heart, provides us with an inspiring start as we reflect on Bible engagement in the context of other faiths and their scriptures. We will limit our discussion here to Islam and the Qur'an but seek to identify guidelines that may help us in our relationships with our neighbours of other world faiths and other sacred texts, whether Jewish, Buddhist, Sikh or Hindu.

Our personal experiences will inevitably shape our responses to this chapter. We may be part of a community in which Muslims and Christians have lived peacefully together for generations, often sharing each other's festivals. On the other hand, our societies may be marked by violent religious conflict. In chapter 4 we explored how our personal experience shapes and can prejudice our understanding of the Bible. It will also shape, and may prejudice, our attitudes to people of other faiths!

What has been your experience of interacting with people of other faiths? Have you ever read the scriptures of another faith, for instance of Islam or Hinduism? If so, in what ways have you discovered these scriptures to be bridges or obstacles in understanding and building relationships with your neighbours of another faith?

Peter Riddell of the Centre for the Study of Islam and Other Faiths at the Bible College of Victoria, Australia, writes of increasing polarization between Christian students of Islam about how best to respond to Muslims.

> At one level there is an increasing divide between the robust approach of former Muslim converts to Christianity and Christians from Islamic countries on one side, versus the much more respectful and irenic approach of many Western Christian specialists on Islam. At another level, Western Christian specialists on Islam are themselves increasingly polarised between robust and irenic approaches to Islam ... At best these differences can be viewed as a healthy feature

of the rich tapestry of Christianity. At worst, they can be seen as weakening Christianity in the face of the increasing challenge from Islam in the West.[123]

These differences of approach and understanding cannot be categorized simply as between Western and non-Western. A more irenic (conciliatory) approach is also represented, for example, among Christians from the developing world serving in Islamic countries – the prayer letters quoted below stand as testimony – and even among some of those who have turned from Islam to become followers of Jesus. In particular, like Sultan Mohammed Paul, they are discovering the fruitful interplay of the Christian and Islamic scriptures and that to read the Bible in a Muslim context can lead to deeper understanding of the Christian story. 'Who shall gauge the debt we may yet have to confess to Islam if that great antagonist prove finally to have compelled us to explore unknown depths of the riches of the revelation of the Triune God?' With these bold words Temple Gairdner, CMS missionary in Egypt, challenged the Pan-Anglican Congress in 1908.[124] It was controversial mission thinking at the time and continues to be so. But a century later, many followers of Jesus serving him in Muslim contexts bear witness that their appreciation of the power and life-related quality of the Bible has indeed been deepened and enriched as they have read it alongside Muslims and witnessed their responses to it.

In recent years a Bible reflection group called *Umma Ruhia* (Spiritual Community) started to meet in a North African country:

> It started with a Muslim family who are friends of one of the couples on our team. They've known each other for three years and work together in a project for handicapped people. Perhaps because of this long friendship and the trust that has developed, the head of the family asked for a meeting where the followers of the Messiah would tell Bible stories and then family members would offer their points of view and reflections from their reading of the Qur'an. What is striking is that as they listen to the Bible stories they are amazed and hungry to hear more[125]

Another letter tells of the day when, thanks to the *Water Is Life* project, piped water first arrived for the inhabitants of a remote village.

> From every house you could hear voices shouting a single phrase, '*Ya el ma!*' ('The water has come!'). Dancing for joy, everyone rushed

to fill containers. People welcomed and blessed me as I visited each family. I went into the mosque – a place not normally open to non-Muslims – to check the water supply there. The imam and his students were full of thanks. As I stood talking with Mustafa, one of the village leaders, I decided to tell him the story of the Good Samaritan to explain that we try to do good through the water project because we seek to live out the teachings of *Sidna Aisa* (the Lord Jesus). 'Now they're going to throw me out of the village,' I thought. But the response was different from anything I had imagined. 'That's an extraordinary story,' said Mustafa. 'Next time you come, please bring me a photocopy of it, and bring it on cassette too, if you can. The whole village needs to hear about this Good Samaritan. I'll give it to the imam so that he can tell this story to all the men.' I was astounded by the response[126]

Three months later comes more news of Mustafa:

We gave him the cassette with the Gospel of Luke recorded on it. Of course it includes the story of the Good Samaritan that had such a powerful impact on him. A few days ago we visited him and his family. He told us that they had all been listening, and because it's the custom here to learn religious texts by heart, they'd started to memorize the whole Gospel. But with so much winding and rewinding, the tape recorder broke. So one of his sons who is studying in the university took the cassette with him and is learning Luke's Gospel by heart. Mustafa's wife has been deeply moved by the story of the life of Jesus – it moves her to tears to hear about him.[127]

Ida Glaser has explored, thoughtfully and convincingly, what God's word, from Genesis to Revelation, has to say about people of other faiths and how God calls us as his followers to relate to them.[128] The Lord's requirements (Mic. 6:8) will be the underlying issue that we consider in this chapter. In the specific context of engaging with the scriptures of other faiths, what does it look like to do justice, love kindness and walk humbly with our God as we consider

- the experience of people of other faiths when they engage with the Bible?
- our response to the scriptures of other faiths?

The Qur'an and Hadith

The Qur'an is the holy book of Islam. Slightly shorter than the New Testament, the Qur'an is divided into 114 *Surah* or 'steps'. The brief first *Surah*, entitled 'The Key' or 'The Opening', provides the words that Muslims pray five times a day:

> 'In the name of Allah, Most Gracious, Most Merciful.
> Praise be to Allah,
> The Cherisher and Sustainer of the Worlds;
> Most Gracious, Most Merciful;
> Master of the Day of Judgement.
> Thee do we worship,
> And Thine aid we seek.
> Show us the straight way,
> The way of those on whom
> Thou hast bestowed Thy Grace,
> Those whose (portion)
> Is not wrath,
> And who go not astray.' [129]

Like the Bible, the Qur'an contains different kinds of writing. In it we will find narrative, much of it with parallels in the Bible, laws and regulations, descriptions of judgment and paradise, and some references to historical events. These writings come together in three main themes: the unity of God, the nature of prophet-hood and the nature of the hereafter. In comparison with the Bible's sense of a narrative that unfolds across several millennia, there is little sense of chronology in the Qur'an. The *Surah* are organized, following the opening one, with the longest near the beginning and the shortest at the end. The *Surah* take their titles from their prominent themes or words. For example, *Surah* 19 is called 'Maryam' (Mary), *Surah* 71 'Nuh' (Noah) and *Surah* 109 'The Unbelievers'. Each *Surah* is divided into verses (*Ayat*). There are about 6,200 verses in the Qur'an.

The Qur'an has been translated from the original Arabic into several languages. One website currently lists eleven, ranging from French to Albanian and Bahasa Malaysia. A translation into Irish was begun in 2003. But the Muslim attitude to the translation of their scriptures is very different from that of Christians, for whom news of a new Bible translation into another language is a source of rejoicing. A note to an English translation of the Qur'an on a Muslim website states, 'This is the English *translation of the meaning* of the Quran [sic], not the Quran itself. The Quran is in its original, pristine Arabic as it was revealed from Allah … One must look into … the original lexical Arabic and scholarly understanding to fully interpret the Quran's meaning.'[130]

The origin of the name 'Qur'an' is the Arabic word *qara'a* meaning 'to recite'. This name reflects the nature of the revelation in which Muslims believe. They hold that the Qur'an is an exact record of the words of Allah eternally engraved on a stone tablet in heaven, spoken over a period of time (AD 622–632) to the prophet Muhammad through the angel Gabriel and written down on different materials – palm leaves, bone and stone. Muslim traditions vary about how the definitive version of the Qur'an came into being. Some hold that Muhammad himself was responsible, others that Abu Bakr, the first caliph, ordered the collection and arrangement of the various writings. Another group credits the third caliph, Uthman, with producing an 'authorized version' towards the end of his reign in AD 656.[131] Muslims, despite the many variations in the faith (Sunni and Shi'a are the two main groups), all read the same Qur'an.

Some groups claim that the Hadith, the extensive collections of traditions about the life and teachings of Muhammad, and Islam's second most sacred scripture, were part of the original Qur'an. The Bukhari edition of the Hadith runs into twelve volumes. Sharia, the formulation of Islamic law, is based partly on commandments in the Qur'an, but far more extensively on the Hadith. As I write this chapter, the media are reporting a radical revision of the Hadith by the Turkish Government's Department of Religious Affairs. Various speakers interviewed on BBC Radio 4's *Today* programme speak of a revision that they believe will return to the pure religion of Muhammad, free of what they describe as the cultural baggage that now obscures its true values. They hold that certain commands, originally intended as temporary measures made for practical reasons, have been turned, for more or less noble motives, into permanent commands. For example, the Hadith's ban on women travelling alone was originally intended as a wise response to the dangers on the roads in Muhammad's time. Elsewhere, Muhammad is quoted as longing for the day when women will be able to travel freely.

It is interesting to follow discussions on various Muslim websites on interpretational issues in both the Qur'an and the Hadith.[132] There is overlap between some of the 'hot' issues for Muslims and for Christians!

For example, exegetes from both faiths continue to search their scriptures for wisdom about the nature and role of women. Another crucial field of Islamic hermeneutics is *jihad* and the understanding of violence in the Qur'an.

When Christians read the Qur'an

If you have never read the Qur'an before, it would be good to do so – at least some of it. It will help you to share something of the experience of the Muslim who reads or listens to the Bible for the first time. You will read the Qur'an through Christian eyes as the Muslim reads the Bible through Muslim eyes (although if you have become a follower of Jesus from a Muslim background, you will read 'bifocally'!). The Qur'an, like the Bible, is available in many bookshops and free to read on the Internet in several different languages.[133]

We have already described the way the material of the Qur'an is organized: while it appears highly structured, there is no sense of an unfolding story, as there is in the Bible. (Readers of the Bible may also struggle to grasp its story line at various points.) A thoughtful reading of the Qur'an makes clear that it is more like a systematic theology dealing with categories such as the unity of God, the nature of God's people, God's ways of guiding human beings, the kind of culture God ordains and the nature of this world and the next.

If you are a Christian reader, it may surprise you to discover that much of the Qur'an will be familiar from your knowledge of the Bible – yet at the same time different. Here you will find Adam, Noah, Abraham, Ishmael, Isaac, Jacob, Moses, Aaron, Elijah, Elisha, Solomon and David, Zechariah and his wife, John the Baptist, Mary and Jesus. Twenty-five biblical characters feature in the Qur'an. One example will illustrate some of the similarities and differences that you will find:

Qur'an, Surah 19 (Mary): 16–21

[16] Relate in the Book
(The story of) Mary,
When she withdrew
From her family
To a place in the East
[17] She placed a screen
(To screen herself) from them;
Then We sent to her
Our angel, and he appeared
Before her as a man
In all respects.
[18] She said: 'I seek refuge
From thee to (Allah)
Most Gracious: (come not near)
If thou dost fear Allah.'
[19] He said: 'Nay, I am only
A messenger from thy Lord,
(To announce) to thee
The gift of a holy son.'
[20] She said: 'How shall I
Have a son, seeing that
No man has touched me,
And I am not unchaste?'
[21] He said: 'So (it will be):
Thy Lord saith, "That is
Easy for Me: and (We
Wish) to appoint him
As a Sign unto men
And a Mercy from Us:
It is a matter
(So) decreed."'[134]

Gospel of Luke 1: 26–35

[26] In the sixth month the angel Gabriel was sent by God to a town in Galilee called Nazareth,
[27] to a virgin engaged to a man whose name was Joseph, of the house of David. The virgin's name was Mary.
[28] And he came to her and said, 'Greetings, favoured one! The Lord is with you.'
[29] But she was much perplexed by his words and pondered what sort of greeting this might be.
[30] The angel said to her, 'Do not be afraid, Mary, for you have found favour with God.
[31] And now, you will conceive in your womb and bear a son, and you will name him Jesus'.
[34] Mary said to the angel, 'How can this be, since I am a virgin?'
[35] The angel said to her, 'The Holy Spirit will come upon you, and the power of the Most High will overshadow you; therefore the child to be born will be holy'.

When we discover what appears to be common ground between our faith and another belief system, we generally react in one of two ways: we can feel 'our' ground is threatened and therefore tend to attack the other belief system, the other version of 'our' story, trying to pull it apart so that we can then start again with our 'pure' version of the truth. Or we can recognize that where there is some common ground, there may be possibilities of building together. Approaches to mission among Muslims have always moved between these two approaches.

Comparing the narrative of Cain and Abel in the Bible (Gen. 4:1–16) and the Qur'an (Surah 5:28–33), Ida Glaser suggests that it can be enlightening for Christians to read the two versions together so as to explore:

- the origins of the two versions (the Qur'anic version may be based on early Jewish commentaries)
- the specific context of the Qur'anic narrative (the story of the two sons of Adam follows material about Jewish covenant breaking and Christian blasphemy; many Muslims understand the story to be about Jewish and Christian opposition to Muslims)
- aspects of the biblical version that we may have overlooked ('the Qur'an focuses on justice for the innocent victim, the Bible focuses on God's interaction with the guilty perpetrator … The biblical "Cain and Abel" makes sense as part of the account of the creation and fall of humankind, which tells at every stage of God's mercy as well as His judgment … It gives us hope that God loves and wants to save the sinner as well as the victim'). Glaser points out that 'Muslims reading this biblical version for the first time are sometimes perturbed that it makes them feel sympathy for the murderer.'[135]

When Muslims read the Bible

Before we even think about how the *content* of the Bible strikes a Muslim, we should be aware that Muslims expect a holy book to be special and treated with reverence. They are often shocked at how Christians seem to treat their Bibles in a casual way – placing them on the floor, underlining or writing notes in them and so on. The Bible Societies and other Bible agencies around the world provide special versions or selections of Scripture that are particularly acceptable to Muslim audiences. These are often referred to as TAZI Scriptures. The title is the acronym for *Tawrat, Anbiya, Zabur* and *Injil* (Arabic for the Law, the Prophets, the Psalms of David and the Gospel of Jesus). TAZI Scriptures feature specially designed covers and beautiful page borders and are usually printed on the cream coloured paper that Muslims believe appropriate for a sacred text.

When Muslims engage with the Bible, what are the main difficulties they may encounter? I remember travelling from London to Edinburgh by bus a few years ago. My neighbour was a young Sudanese Muslim from Khartoum, visiting his sister who was studying medicine in Scotland. He had just bought a Bible and was starting to explore it. I learned a lot on that journey about the things that were puzzling and even shocking him as he read, but also about his fascination with what he perceived as common ground. Here is a brief outline of four of the obstacles he had encountered.

1. The understanding of revelation

Both Muslims and Christians believe that God has revealed himself, his character and purposes, to humankind. Both faiths believe that he has done so by communicating to faithful persons the one crucial message that human beings need to hear and pass on. But there are major differences between Islam and Christianity about the nature of revelation. As we have seen, the Qur'an is generally understood among orthodox Muslims, not as a product of human intelligence or inspiration, but as God's message revealed word for word to the prophet Muhammad through the angel Gabriel, recorded by Muhammad's companions and transmitted through the generations. 'No Muslim would accept any other view than that the Qur'an came verbatim from heaven.'[136] As we noted in chapter 3, there are Christians who hold to a rather similar understanding of a 'dictated' Bible (see page 36).

When a Muslim encounters the Bible he discovers a very different kind of record from what he is familiar with in the Qur'an.

> Muslims who address themselves to the Bible find a variety of books of independent authorship, stretching over more than a millennium … It is difficult [for them] to comprehend why there should be four Gospels, when the Gospel, or *Injil*, entrusted by God to Jesus the Prophet, was a single book, though now no longer extant. The assumption is immediate that because there are four, none of them is valid.[137]

The Muslim Bible reader will come across texts such as, 'Now the acts of King David … are written in the records of the seer Samuel, and in the records of the prophet Nathan, and in the records of the seer Gad' (1 Chron. 29:29). This evidence of multiple authorship is quite different from the Qur'an's record. In the New Testament, again, Muslims discover different people each claiming to bring God's word: 'This is the disciple who is testifying to these things and has written them, and we know that his testimony is true' (John 21:24) and 'I too decided, after investigating everything carefully … to write an orderly account for you, most excellent Theophilus, so that you may know the truth' (Luke 1:3, 4).

There is in fact some degree of diversity of understanding of Qur'anic revelation among Muslim scholars. Fazlur Rahman, for example, writes that, 'the Qur'an is entirely the Word of God and, in an ordinary sense, also entirely the Word of Muhammad'.[138] In the fifteenth century, the famed Muslim historian Ibn Khaldun claimed that the Qur'an 'differs from the Torah, the Gospel and the other heavenly books. The prophets received their books in the form of ideas during the state of revelation. After their return to a human state, they expressed those ideas in their own ordinary words.'[139] Steven Masood comments that while this comes close to the Christian understanding of how God interacted with the Bible writers, there are nevertheless significant differences between the Islamic concept of passive 'received revelations' given to one prophet, and the Christian understanding of the 'God-breathed' quality of the records of the forty or so Bible writers who so often give evidence of their active involvement in the project, as in the case of Luke's 'orderly account' that we have mentioned.[140]

2. The nature of prophets

As we have seen, many of the Old Testament's 'heroes' or 'prophets', as Islam refers to them, appear also in the Qur'an. But there are aspects of the biblical version of their stories that are likely to disturb many Muslims who have grown up in the tradition of regarding the prophets as *masoom*, innocent. These men are characterized by complete trustworthiness, protected by God from wrongdoing and disease. So biblical accounts of, for example, Moses' murder of the Egyptian (Exod. 2:12) or David's adultery with Bathsheba (2 Sam. 11) can make it difficult for a Muslim to give attention to other, more important aspects of their stories. 'They said that Jesus drank wine and told his disciples to drink wine. I can't believe that of so great a prophet!' For a Muslim father attending an Easter presentation at his daughter's school in the UK, this information had shock value that overrode everything that was said about the resurrection of Jesus.[141]

Nevertheless the Qur'an itself records many instances of the prophets asking God for mercy and forgiveness. For example, *Surah* 38:17–26 contains material that is parallel to the prophet Nathan's challenge to David after his adultery with Bathsheba (2 Sam. 12:1–15), though there is no mention in the Qur'an of David's adultery:

> 'And David gathered that We
> Had tried him: he asked
> Forgiveness of his Lord,
> Fell down, bowing
> (In prostration), and turned
> (To Allah in repentance).'[142]

It is interesting to reflect how often in our Bible work with children, we 'sanitize' certain Bible stories and actually communicate a version of the lives of the fallible men and women through whom God chose to work that is actually closer to the Qur'an's version than the Bible's! (See pp. 102,103.)

3. The identity of Jesus as the 'Son of God'

As the testimony at the start of this chapter makes clear, Islam honours Jesus, the sinless Prophet. The Qur'an speaks of Issa, the Messiah, the Son of Mary, Prophet, Servant, Word of God etc. There are around thirty-five references to him in the Qur'an, including two accounts of his birth in *Surah* 3 and 19. It can be a shock to Christians to understand how Islam's honouring of Jesus can be turned into attack on the Christian portrayal of him: 'The Koran [sic] in fact exalts "Issa" more than the Gospel does. For the Gospel casts a shadow over Jesus' morality, presenting him not only as a wine-drinker but even as one who multiplied wine at the wedding-feast of Cana.'[143]

Even more problematic for Muslim readers of the Bible is what it has to say about the nature of Jesus' relationship with God, and what it implies about his participation in the Trinity. Muslims express dismay at the idea of the Trinity and revulsion at what they understand to be the Christian belief that God united with Mary in sexual union. Steven Masood warns, 'If we tell our Muslim friend "Jesus is the Son of God" this may reinforce his belief that Christians blasphemously believe in three gods (Muslims think the Trinity consists of God, Mary and their son Jesus).'[144] The Qur'an denies repeatedly that God can have children. The brief statement in *Surah* 112 is perhaps the best-known expression of this doctrine:

> In the name of Allah, Most Gracious, Most Merciful.
> Say: he is Allah,
> The One and Only;
> Allah, the Eternal, Absolute;
> He begetteth not,

Nor is He begotten;
And there is none
Like unto Him.[145]

There is also the very explicit *Surah* 4:171:

O People of the Book!
Commit no excesses
In your religion: nor say
Of Allah aught but the truth.
Christ Jesus the son of Mary
Was (no more than)
A Messenger of Allah,
And His Word,
Which He bestowed on Mary,
And a Spirit proceeding
From Him: so believe
In Allah and His Messengers.
Say not "Trinity": desist:
It will be better for you:
For Allah is One God:
Glory be to Him:
(Far Exalted is He) above
Having a son.[146]

But Muslims reading the Gospels will hear Jesus pray, 'I thank you Father, Lord of heaven and earth … All things have been handed over to me by my Father; and no one knows the Son except the Father, and no one knows the Father except the Son' (Matt. 11:25, 27). In John's Gospel, they will find the most frequent use of the title 'Son of God' and even more problematically, Jesus' words to Nicodemus, 'God … gave his only Son' (John 3:16).

Friendship with Muslims challenges us to be more careful about how we talk about God – and perhaps to find this not simply an intellectual challenge but a journey of discovery taking us closer to our one God whom we know as Father, Son and Holy Spirit. Kenneth Cragg encourages us, in seeking to interpret our faith to Muslims, to 'begin with this plea that the Muslim estimate and ponder the Christian Trinity not as a violation of unity, but as a form of its expression … we are both firmly and equally believers that God is one.'[147]

4. The death of Jesus

> That they said (in boast),
> "We killed Christ Jesus
> The son of Mary,
> The Messenger of Allah: –
> But they killed him not,
> Nor crucified him,
> But so it was made
> To appear to them …
> For of a surety
> They killed him not –
> Nay, Allah raised him up
> Unto Himself [148]

This unequivocal denial of the Bible's account of the death of Jesus in *Surah* 4:157, 158 is perhaps the central challenge to Christians reading the Qur'an and engaging with Muslims who are encountering the New Testament's accounts of the crucifixion. The Islamic presupposition is that for prophets such as Moses and David, failure and ignominy are unthinkable. How much more, then, is a shameful death unthinkable for the Messenger of Allah. 'The Qur'anic teaching is that Christ was not crucified nor killed by the Jews, notwithstanding certain apparent circumstances which produced that illusion in the minds of some of his enemies … Allah raised him up (*rafa'a*) to Himself.' [149]

Kenneth Cragg warns Christians against arrogant or argumentative responses to Muslim rejection of the cross: 'We must affirm the fact of the Cross always in the same spirit in which Jesus himself suffered it.' [150] He proposes some approaches that may encourage Muslims to find more common ground in the Bible's account of the death of Jesus. For example, the Gospels bear witness to the cross as the outcome of the hostility that Jesus experienced from those who opposed his message and his actions. While the Qur'an is silent on the content of Jesus' teaching, one of the themes it has in common with the Bible is the hostility experienced by all God's prophets. However, Cragg is also realistic about how a Muslim person's understanding of the nature of God makes it almost impossible, in human terms, for him to accept the Bible's account of Jesus' self-giving: 'It must be remembered that the Muslim rewriting of the crucifixion story is thought to be in the interests of God's glory. God, it is held, cannot be honoured in the victory of a prophet's foes.'[151] The testimony at the start of this chapter tells us that the Holy Spirit can bring about just such a radical new understanding!

As we think about our relationships with people of other faiths and their scriptures, we return, as we have often done in this book, to the Emmaus road (Luke 24). Yes, it may be important for us to read the Qur'an or the Vedas or even the Book of Mormon and to reflect on these scriptures in the light of God's unique word. But as Jesus did on the road that evening, we must also learn to walk alongside our Muslim or Hindu or Sikh neighbours and *listen* to the conversations that are already going on among them. Our relationships will be marked by empathy. In anything we may have to say about Scripture, we will make authentic connections with what our neighbour shares with us. Most importantly of all, we will go beyond sharing words to sharing our lives. 'The final urge to Christian mission is what Christ is and what, because of him, we know God to be. We must represent the Gospel of Christ in the spirit and fellowship of him from whom it derives.'[152]

7

Young Word

Keep these words ... Recite them to your children and talk about them

— **Deuteronomy 6:6, 7**

2007 was the bicentennial of the abolition of the slave trade in Britain. Up and down the country, schools focused on our shameful history of slavery and on the abolitionist campaigning of William Wilberforce, Olaudah Equiano, John Newton and others. In one primary school children learned that slaves were forced either to change their African birth names or to have a number tattooed on their arms. This information so shocked one little girl that she went to her teacher and asked if all her class might, in a small way, enter into the slaves' experience of enforced anonymity (though she didn't put it quite like that!). For two weeks children and teachers also became nameless, using only the numbers stencilled on their arms to address each other. So powerful was this experience – however partial – of one aspect of slave life that the whole school eventually became involved in supporting the Anti-Slavery Society that works to protect children and other vulnerable groups from exploitation. A single detail of the information she received in school about the slave trade engaged this child's mind and heart and prompted her to take action. Her involvement with the slaves' story then drew the whole school into an active response that went beyond anything her teachers had imagined![153]

This seems to me to be a model of what we pray for when we encourage children and young people – and adults too – to engage with God's word. We want them to go beyond merely accumulating biblical information to interaction with Scripture that involves the whole person and brings about both individual and communal transformation. God's story, like the story of slavery, has the potential to intrigue children and engage them at every level. This is a crucial aspect of opening the Bible with the younger generation that we will explore in this chapter.

One chapter can't do justice to all that could be said, for example, about appropriate models of Bible engagement for different levels of child development. There are significant differences between helpful approaches for children of ten to twelve years old and less and those of, say, eleven to eighteen years. For example, the ability to think in abstract terms is not usually found in children under the age of eleven.

The Bible and children in the church community

Children's experience of the Bible within the setting of the church usually falls into one of two categories. Either the Bible is handled like an important school textbook, a source of information and data to memorize, or it is 'managed' as a problematic and dull text that needs to be mediated to children through entertaining activities. I don't want to suggest that there is no place for teaching Scripture to children or no place for enjoyment in the process of engaging with the Bible; far from it, as we shall see in a later section of this chapter. But both of these approaches, if used without thought and care, can prevent children from experiencing the Bible as a place of true and transforming encounter with God. Here is how an experienced children's minister describes the two approaches. First, an overly didactic, educational approach to bringing the Bible and children together:

> When we use the Bible with children simply to teach doctrinal tenets, moral absolutes, tips for better living, or stories of heroes to be emulated, we stunt the spiritual formation of our children and deprive them of the valuable, spiritual story of God. When we only distil the Bible into practical applications and little life lessons, we fail to teach children how to use the Bible as a means of understanding God's overarching purposes in the world. We fail to give them the ability to understand their own stories in light of God's story. When we tell them what the Bible says or what to believe about what a particular Bible passage says, we rob them of the ability to experience the text for themselves and pull out its meaning in their own context and the larger context of their world. These are far

> more valuable spiritual skills for the child than learning Bible facts
> or spiritual axioms.[154]

Some of our favourite Christian education tactics may need re-evaluation in the light of this thinking. For example, do we tend to use a lot of Bible quizzes or competitions to review material we have taught? If so, what kind of questions are we asking the children? The names of Joseph's brothers? The kind of tree that Zacchaeus climbed? How many times Noah sent out a bird from the ark? Or do we ask questions that actually enable children to reflect on the God they have met in these stories and his interaction with human beings? Do we help them to explore the nature of the God whom Joseph learned painfully to trust? Do we encourage them to feel how Zacchaeus felt as he responded to Jesus' surprising, 'I'm coming home with you today'? Do we dare to encourage our children to explore what the flood and the ark were really all about – or do we leave them with a nursery story of animals going in two by two?

What, then, of the entertainment-focused approach?

> Many church-based children's Bible-teaching programs consist of entertaining interludes that pass for religious education. The passive children sit watching puppets, skits, videos and sleight-of-hand illusions based on the Bible, Bible stories, or Bible characters. The children may interact from time to time with what's happening onstage ... or they may get up to jump around while singing songs about 'pumping it up for Jesus' ... Naturally children enjoy this, but I don't believe their spiritual lives or their experience with God is enhanced through these kinds of programs. There is little interaction with adult members of the faith community or the other children. There is no opportunity to wonder about or play with the Bible story. While these programs can seem wonderfully creative and child friendly, they do little to help children meet the God of the Bible and understand how to live as God's people.[155]

Commenting on both approaches to helping children to engage with God's word. Emmanuel Todjo describes the situation in the churches of Cameroon, where he reports that children are expected to recite the lesson without reflecting on any real-life implications of what they have heard from Scripture. The outcome has been 'Christians' whose lifestyle contradicts the gospel. When Scripture Union in Cameroon started to implement the Aid for Aids programme in schools, staff soon realized that the young people knew all the right answers, but in personal conversations they were willing to admit that in real life, things were very different: '90% of young people answered that the best way to avoid AIDS is abstinence and faithfulness. In fact 44% admitted to being sexually active and 32% said they would continue because they simply don't know how to stop.' Of his own practice of the entertainment approach to engaging children with the Bible, Emmanuel Todjo admits with irony that, 'Before I encountered the Lord, I was a much-appreciated Sunday school teacher. In reality, though, I was helping children to play, without making any connection to the Lord Jesus. Even my lessons were just an introduction to jokes and entertainment.'[156]

Before reading further, take time to reflect on how children in your society and church community experience the Bible. To what extent would you describe that experience as 'educational' or 'entertaining' or something else? What changes, if any, would you like to see?

So what might a third way look like, an approach that encourages our children to enter with mind, heart and imagination into Scripture as God's story, his revelation of himself as sovereign Lord, God in three Persons, all his energies bent on the healing and renewal of the whole creation? This is a question that needs a lot of unpacking. In this chapter I simply want to point us towards some of the thinking that people with a lot of experience in children's ministry are coming up with. In Appendix 1 you will find books and other resources that explore these ideas in more detail.

- In our telling of Bible stories, we need to focus always on what the narrative tells us about God and how he relates to the world and the people he has created. Our aim is to enable children to *discover for themselves* the relevance of God's story for their lives. Of course to do this, we need to be involved in the same discovery process for ourselves! The Bible talks about life in the most realistic terms for young people – about peer pressure, dysfunctional families, image, sex, rebellion, money, inter-generational strains, competition, loneliness, failure – as well as joy, love, fulfilment, beauty and so on. So we won't offer children a sanitized version of the Bible or one in which we tell selective versions of God's activity in the lives of its 'heroes' and 'heroines'. Of course we must consider the stages of a child's development and what is appropriate for what stage. But we should not be telling children anything that we later have to un-tell them. This is likely to undermine their confidence in God's word. The story of David tells how God gave him courage to face Goliath but it also tells how God didn't turn a blind eye to his adultery with Bathsheba and murder of her husband.

- Rather than providing pre-packaged 'answers', we should seek to *intrigue* children so that they want to explore more about God, more about Jesus.

- We need to be ready to admit that we don't have all the answers ourselves, that there may be parts of the Bible that we struggle with. Sometimes children's questions can provoke us into doing some more careful reflection!

- We can help children to 'inhabit' the Bible story, to engage their imagination, to hear, see, smell and feel it. It was the apparently small detail of the slaves' tattooed numbers that triggered the response of the little girl whose story opens this chapter.

- We can imitate Jesus' way of telling stories – often, indeed usually, allowing his listeners to work out the meaning of his parables for themselves. Don't be afraid to be open-ended in telling Bible stories, expecting God's Spirit to speak to the children, rather than informing them what the 'life application' of the story is.

- We should make it clear that we value and welcome the insights of children and young people about the Bible. Be prepared to accept any honest response from them. A group of teachers of religious education in Australia told one of my colleagues that their most honest answers and comments invariably came from non-Christian children who didn't know the 'right' answers. The boy who responded to Joseph's refusal to be seduced by Potiphar's wife with the comment, 'Miss, I think he's an idiot!' was doing so on the basis of his life experience – the TV he watched, the conversations he had with his friends, maybe his own family situation.[157] When a reply like this is properly received it can open the door to authentic exploration of how God's word addresses our lives.

- We can help children to appreciate the different kinds of literature in the Bible – poetry, proverbs, letters, as well as narrative. Deliberately aim to handle these different texts in different ways. For example, exploration of a psalm might include encouraging children to write a poem or song or rap of their own. Adolescents might engage with the psalms like the entries in a spiritual journal, poems and songs that bring together life experience and relationship with God. Enable children to encounter as wide a range as possible of the different types of Bible literature. Too many children's ministers are reluctant to range beyond the four Gospels when they consider their Christian education or holiday Bible club programme. Biblical material that is not clearly narrative fills them with alarm! Surely children won't be interested in prophecy or the New Testament letters? And in any case, how could these be evangelistic? Two of the most effective and memorable Bible activity programmes for camping holidays that I have been involved in took young teens through the experiences of Jeremiah and explored Paul's letter to the Ephesians. The artificial division we often make between Bible engagement for evangelism and for discipleship is an unhelpful one, untrue to Scripture itself. If we are helping young people to experience the Bible as a place where God speaks to them, then we can trust that he will speak according to the needs of each child. The good news starts with Genesis and continues to Revelation, it is not limited to the Passion accounts in the four Gospels! In her work with young people in Australia Naomi Swindon encourages them to explore through interactive Bible engagement the richness of the God she wants them to know – as Creator, Sustainer, Imaginer of beauty, Embodier of upside-down values, Good Boss, Passionate Lover, Jilted Lover, Reconciler, Rescuer, Parent, Promise-Keeper. Exploration like this takes young people off the beaten track in the Bible – into Hosea and the Song of Songs, into Romans, Ruth and Jeremiah. They don't get bored![158]

- We should make opportunities for children and young people to experience what the Bible text is describing. I have vivid memories of taking teenagers out on a calm moonlit night during a camp in Bolivia. We climbed to the top of a hill and listened to one of the young people read Psalm 8: 'When I look at your heavens … the moon and the stars that you have established; what are human beings that you are mindful of them? … O Lord … how majestic is your name in all the earth!' There was quiet as the reading ended, the young people silenced by the same awe of God's creation and his care that had moved the psalmist to worship. In Melbourne, a youth worker takes teenagers to different parts of the city to listen to readings from the Gospels. In the financial district, they will hear Jesus invite a man of great wealth to sell everything, give his money to the poor and come and follow him. In the red light district, they ponder Jesus' welcome of a woman 'who was a sinner' and her rejection by polite society.

- We need to be bold about deliberately letting children experience something very different in their engagement with the Bible from either school or entertainment. Ivy Beckwith relates how she has used the ancient practice of Lectio Divina with a group of primary-age children. She encourages the children to sit quietly and listen to the reading of a short passage of the Bible. The passage will be read two or three times. The children respond by sharing what has 'jumped out' of the reading for them, what thoughts have come to them about what they've heard:

> Now we have no way of knowing what is going on in their heads as they reflect on the Bible story being read to them, but in my experience they do become engaged in the process and respond … without silliness and sometimes with profundity. Children can do silence … And as they practice Lectio, I believe God speaks to them through the text of Scripture in ways that are meaningful to them because that is what God desires to do.[159]

- 'Godly Play' is a similar approach to Bible engagement with children that many churches around the world have discovered in recent years. It encourages children to listen to carefully narrated Bible stories as they sit together with the leader on the floor. The leader uses simple visual aids (a sand box, wooden figures, hand gestures) and then invites children to reflect on what they have heard by means of 'I wonder …' questions ('I wonder how Abraham felt as he set out into the desert with his family'; 'I wonder why Peter said he didn't know Jesus'). Such questions help the children to feel that the leader, rather than knowing all the 'answers', is exploring the significance of the narrative along with them. After this exploration, children are encouraged to choose from a range of activities to respond to what they have heard. They can paint or draw or retell the Bible story to themselves, using the same visual aids. They may write a prayer or design a symbol that summarizes what God has told them through the story. Or they may simply choose to be quiet and think about what they have heard.[160]

- Be bold about encouraging children to listen even to long narrative passages of the Bible. In camps for primary children in New Zealand, leaders have read the Gospels and even parts of the Old Testament with youngsters and been amazed and delighted to discover some children back in their cabins or tents, reading on in their Bibles, 'because we want to know what happens next!'[161] An experienced children's worker reports that 'children want to find their own way around the Bible and read about God for themselves ... children who struggle to read a sentence yet ask in every lesson if they can find the passage we are using in their own Bible, and then faithfully mark it with anything that will serve as a bookmark.'[162]
- Take seriously every aspect of the formation of those involved in the spiritual nurture of children. The people who minister to young people in our churches need an understanding of how they think and react at different stages of life. They also need insight into what young people are watching and listening to, and how their values are being shaped. Their own relationship with God and his word is of course at the heart of everything they will do with the children.

> Lack of training, no knowledge of how children reason and learn, and little class preparation are a recipe for really bad Bible teaching. This does little to help today's children see the Bible and God's stories as relevant to their lives, culture, and ultimately the world. It's no wonder that surveys and polls of college students raised in the church show these students having little or no knowledge of the stories of the Bible and no way of making the intellectual, affectual and behavioural leaps to see what living as a person of faith in God looks like in the real world.[163]

Hermeneutics matter!

A strange double standard often operates when it comes to issues of interpreting the Bible in the context of ministry to children. People who would normally be quick to point out what they consider to be inappropriate understandings of the Bible in a sermon to adults, seem happy to use questionable hermeneutical approaches with children. It seems that the root of this practice is our sense that the Bible is a difficult text, distant from our experience, and even more distant from the experience of our children. It has therefore to be tamed and controlled and mediated to the children, as we have already seen, by an educational process or by turning it into something entertaining. We can sometimes be so concerned to contextualize the Bible into the world of the child that we fail completely to take seriously the other key hermeneutical contexts – especially that of the Bible authors. We have already mentioned how the standard handling with children of the story of Noah and the flood tends to focus on the cosier aspects and largely ignores the issues of God's grief over human wickedness and his decision to deal drastically with violence and corruption. That is to say, our focus with children tends to shift from God's revelation of himself to the apparently more acceptable details of the human story.

> When we show children the Bible as simply a book given for their amusement and entertainment, we may end up with children who have a view of God as the merry master (with Jesus as his erstwhile sidekick) of the universe who simply wants us to be cheerful, kind, and nice to other people. The stories of God are much more than that.[164]

Everything that we have considered in chapter 4 about careful hermeneutics needs to be taken seriously in our work with children – in fact even more seriously because children are not usually in a position to challenge our interpretations of Scripture. As we mentioned earlier in this chapter, we should not be teaching children anything that we later have to un-teach them. In other words, we should not use cosy, amusing, reduced understandings of the Bible narrative that our children will have to come to terms with (or not come to terms with) later as the offensive texts that we talked about in chapter 5.

Glenn Cupit, an Australian educator and child development specialist, offers us a helpful model for thinking about children, how they interpret the Bible and how we may need to think about our interpretational practice as we work with children. Pointing out that adults more often than not rush to explain to children what a Bible passage 'means', he argues that children

> approach life as an experience to be emotionally and relationally lived, not as a set of logical propositions to be rationally solved ... I suggest that 'meaning' consists of more than words and ideas and is also derived from processes other than logical analysis. Children do not learn to be like their parents by analysing their nature, forming a conceptual map of their characteristics and identifying what they

must do to emulate those categories. (Any more than adults can use that process to fulfil Jesus' requirement that they become like children.) The process is far more visceral and intuitive. The Bible is inspired, not to allow us to develop a systematic theology, but to bring us into relationship with God.[165]

Cupit proposes what he calls a 'ladder' of ways through which human beings discover meaning in all of life and specifically in the Bible. The eight 'rungs' of the ladder, starting with the earliest and most universal experiences, are:

context

implication

conception

personal relevance/identification

familiarity/memory

imagination

emotion

enjoyment/aesthetics

None of these ways of exploring the meaning for us of God's word ever becomes irrelevant to us, though the first 'rungs' of the ladder of meaning are where children are likely to feel most at home. We move onto the higher rungs as we develop and have more experience of interacting with God's word.

Cupit explores how we can encourage children to move on from one level to the next of understanding and interpreting the Bible. The process may start with the **enjoyment** of a parent or other significant adult reading or narrating Scripture to children from their earliest years, with no attempt to 'apply' the material. Enjoyment of Scripture is likely to be powerfully associated with the warmth of key relationships. Cupit then suggests that:

> The Bible is an intensely **emotional** book ... If one reads the Bible without recognising its emotional force and being deeply moved, in many different ways, one has not read it with understanding ... We must expect children to be moved by the stories ... our relationship with God is quintessentially emotional: fear is the beginning of wisdom and love its outcome; joy is a fruit of the Spirit.[166]

The church therefore needs skilled story tellers as well as teachers. We have to be ready to accept children's emotional reactions to God's word and help them to reflect on their feelings as authentic spiritual responses.

We have already touched on the level of children's **imaginative engagement** with the Bible. We've heard Ivy Beckwith's plea to allow children to wonder at and play with the Bible stories, identifying with the characters, imagining how they may feel and what they may want. In chapter 3 we explored the role of imagination in encouraging response to God's word, not only in children, but in adults too (p. 33).

The fourth means by which children expand their horizons of biblical meaning, is that of **memory**. We probably remember our favourite childhood stories, books that our parents had to read time after time, or videos that got worn out with viewing. Children can also develop this same affectionate familiarity with the Bible, helped by our, 'D'you remember what happened next?' questions, or Bible verses set to memorable tunes.

The fifth stage is the significant moment when a child recognizes that these Bible words resonate with his or her experience. This can vary from a child's powerful **identification** of him or herself with a Bible character, to an unfocused understanding that the Bible content 'makes sense' and even to what Cupit calls 'life-changing self-reorganisation'.[167]

Cupit warns against making premature demands of children for **conceptual engagement** with the Bible – that is, demands to express their discoveries in the Bible and about God in *abstract* terms, such as justice or peace or forgiveness: '[Children] need to be allowed to use their intuition in comprehending scripture and to supplement that with logic as that ability develops from a basic capacity in middle childhood to developed reasoning in adolescence (at least for some).'[168]

Helping children to engage with the Bible at the level of **implication** is fraught with dangers! How quick we adults are to tell children how they should behave in the light of the day's Bible passage – and how slow, usually, we are as adults to practise what we preach! Cupit warns of the trap of finding a 'so that' in every Bible passage and advises the practice of encouraging children to reflect for themselves on the possible implications of the text, refusing to push or manipulate children into responses. Those ministering to children from other faith backgrounds need to be especially careful not to press children into specific action in response to Scripture: Elisha's permission to Naaman to take part in pagan worship (2 Kgs 5:15–19) is an interesting and relevant case study![169]

The skills of understanding Scripture in terms of its **context** – textual, canonical, authorial – take a lifetime to develop. As we have seen, adults can sometimes be keener to push irrelevant contextual information at children than they are to give children the freedom to do their own exploring of a Bible text. Helping children understand Bible context involves not answering questions children are not asking! It *does* involve helping young people to appreciate the differences between poetry and narrative and how to respond differently to them; it may include giving them factual information about Jews and Samaritans or providing a map of Palestine in the time of Jesus. It certainly involves creative approaches that will help children and young people (and indeed adults) to grasp how the Big Story of the Bible fits together. You'll find one suggestion for doing that in chapter 8 (page 115).

Children and the Bible at home

When the apostle Paul wrote to his young disciple and friend Timothy, he was quick to acknowledge the influence of Timothy's home life in his spiritual development. His grandmother Lois and mother Eunice were both women of faith. The same faith in Jesus had been born in Timothy and nurtured from his earliest years by reflection on Scripture (2 Tim. 1:5; 3:14, 15). The Old Testament too tells us a story of the need for faithful communication of God's ways across the generations: 'And when your children ask you, "What do you mean by this observance?" you shall say, "It is the passover sacrifice to the Lord"' (Exod. 12:26, 27; cf. Deut. 6:6, 7).

It's impossible to overstate how important the support and encouragement of adults can be for a child, in nurturing interest in reading or listening to God's word. For many children, the key adults in this process will be parents who have discovered the resources of Scripture for themselves and long to pass on the story of God to their children. Or it may be a grandparent or an older brother or sister who has come to faith. What is crucial is that the adults or older siblings are *themselves* discovering God in the Bible and living in ways that are coherent with God's word. Children are quick to notice when an adult's behaviour doesn't match the word by which he says he lives.

> We will never convince [our children] that the Bible is refreshing, vital and full of adventure if we don't find it so, if we have never longed for God with a godly dissatisfaction and found him with the help of the Bible's pages.[170]

To read or listen to Scripture each day with our children will, in some cultures, be a normal Christian practice. For many African Christians (perhaps more among rural communities than in the cities), the day starts early with 'Morning Glory' or its equivalent – songs of worship, the reading of Scripture and prayer. In many other cultures, including my own, any form of family prayers today is counter-cultural. I sometimes stay with the family of a colleague here in the UK. Some of my best memories of visiting are of informal family prayers at the breakfast table. One of the younger children will cheerfully read the day's passage – breathlessly and sometimes interrupting with a perplexed question ('Dad, wasn't it unfair of Jesus to send the pigs into the sea?'). Questions and comments are welcomed and taken seriously. Everyone is encouraged to talk with God in brief prayers. These may express discoveries about God, puzzlement, joys and anxieties about the day ahead, love and concern for school friends and family. This commitment to listening to God's word together, within the context of the fun and affection of life together, has built trust and communication between parents and children that has sustained them through some rough times. I don't want to give the impression of some smooth, model Christian family. The pressures of busy lives and multiple activities and the moods of different family members can make prayers a struggle. But in some important way their counter-cultural practice is refreshing and encouraging for those who from time to time can share it.

The form of family prayer time will vary from culture to culture. In some cultures it will always be the father or grandfather who presides over family worship. Some may believe it inappropriate for children to read Scripture or pray. It's important for us all to reflect on our practice and ask what light Scripture itself may shed on the way we do things. Are we only reflecting the values of our culture? Might we do things in a different way, a more Christ-like way? We remember the importance that Jesus himself always gave to children, and his call to us to be child-like in relating to him and his kingdom (Luke 9:47, 48; Matt. 18:3). We can miss out on the beauty and richness of children's insights if we don't draw them in to our times of family worship and Bible reflection.

The suggestions listed below seem to be appropriate across all cultures to the practice of family prayers:

- Use a version of the Bible that children find easy to understand.

- Try to establish a clear but relaxed routine – children need to understand that you think this time with God is important. But don't be legalistic about it.
- If they can read, encourage your children to contribute by reading the passage for the family. Sometimes you can vary the routine by listening to Scripture on cassette or CD.
- Let your children share in the privileges of reading the Bible passage, choosing worship songs and praying.
- Be realistic about the length of the Bible passage and try to build children's understanding of how the whole Bible fits together.
- Encourage your children to ask questions about the passage and share their insights. Prompt everyone to explore possible answers, rather than always offering your own.
- By your own questions and comments, encourage your children to be growing in their understanding of who God is and how they can relate to him. Try to avoid right/wrong questions or questions that have yes/no answers. Remember the value of 'I wonder …' questions.
- Pray that your children will develop a love for God's word.
- Pray for yourselves as parents, that by the grace of God and in the power of the Spirit, your words and actions and attitudes will model God's ways to your children.

When we think about young people's earliest experience of the Bible, we need also to consider those who don't have a home or parents who value and love God's word. We think of Christian orphanages, drop-in centres for young people and projects that seek to reach out with the love of Jesus to street children or child labourers. In all these situations the attitude of adult leaders and volunteers to the Bible will be crucial for forming attitudes to God's word in the children. We should consider whether reading from the Bible text is most appropriate, or perhaps using some of the many audio Scripture resources, some of them superbly dramatized. There are specially developed Bible-focused materials that may be helpful for children who live on the streets, children who cannot read or for whom the idea of expressing an opinion on a Bible text that has been read is quite alien. Websites such as www.curbsproject.org.uk and www.lifewords.info (follow the links to Pavement Project) offer resources to help 'urban priority' children and children at risk to discover God's love and care in his word. But no amount of creative resources will take the place of the adult leader or volunteer who loves and lives by God's word, handles it wisely and seeks to help a child to discover how his or her story is present within God's story in Scripture.

Encouragement to persevere

I realize that for many people reading this book, this chapter may sound hopelessly idealistic. Perhaps you are struggling with under-resourced children's ministry in church; you may feel a failure because your own children have no interest in engaging with the Bible. There are no quick-fix solutions, but you may be encouraged by this story from Peru.

The boys who live on the streets of Lima and other cities find it hard to trust anyone – even those who seek to care for them. How can they believe a good God loves them when they are so often told that they are the scum of the earth and treated abusively? The team at a Christian residential centre in downtown Lima takes a carefully low-key approach to introducing these boys to the story of God. At bedtime someone will read a short Bible passage, usually with little or no comment and with a silent prayer. Normally there will be no response from the boys. But one evening a few years ago staff were taken aback to realize that the boys were crying as they listened to the evening's Bible reading. It was Mark's account of the trial of Jesus and his silence in the face of harsh questioning by powerful people (Mark 14:53–65). Hesitantly the boys began to talk about how they identified with the Jesus they met in this story. When they are arrested and questioned under pressure, these street boys choose to keep silence. They do so to protect the thoughts and feelings that are often all that they can call their own: 'This is our story ... Our silence is our truth. This Jesus is one of us.'[171]

8

Church's Word

God's word ... at work in you believers
— 1 Thessalonians 2:13

A washing line, lots of clothes pegs and a simple wooden cross: this was all the equipment Sister Teresa needed to draw a group of people into the storyline of the Bible. She was a Catholic nun whose role in this Bolivian parish was to encourage *lectura popular de la Biblia* – grassroots or community Bible reading. I watched her stretch the rope across the floor and place the cross about two-thirds of the way along it. Her audience was made up of ordinary people from the neighbourhood – shopkeepers, housewives, truck drivers, school children. No priests, no professors.

> When we come together to reflect on God's word, it helps if we understand how one part of the story relates to another. The Bible is a big story, spanning about two thousand years of history and told to us in a whole library of books! The cross here marks the day when Jesus died for us outside Jerusalem. But what about the story of the weeks and months and years – even centuries – before and after that day when Jesus died? If we help one another we'll start to remember what happened and who did what. We can all think of someone who's in God's story – people like Abraham and Ruth, Peter and Mary and John the Baptist. Or we can remember something that happened, like the Exodus or the wedding in Cana. Let's write these names and events down on bits of paper and peg them on the line in the order we think they come in the story.

This warm and unthreatening approach encouraged the most timid members of the group. Even those who muttered, '*Ay, no sé nada...*' ('Oh dear, I don't know anything...') were soon chatting together, scribbling on bits of paper or asking others to write for them, and discussing where to peg their contributions along the rope. Those who could read and had Bibles with them helped those who didn't. After half an hour or so the washing line was crowded with names and events, and people sat back, surprised and delighted that they could remember so much when they worked together.[172]

Sister Teresa taught me a lot that day. She was a brilliant facilitator of interactive, discovery learning. She loved God's word and believed deeply that this word is for *everyone*, not just for those who have been to seminary or got a degree. *Everyone* was capable of exploring Scripture and experiencing its power to change lives and communities. As the day's activities unfolded she encouraged people to make connections between what was happening in the neighbourhood and the Bible's story, and to reflect on how God's word 'read' the life of the community, suggested alternative possibilities and empowered people to live differently:

> The word is gathering together and creating a community, and the community in its turn offers the environment, the context, for the reading of the word. Someone defined the base ecclesial communities as 'the people gathering to look for Christ's word'.[173]

The church: a community forged by God's word

The biblical narrative that we pieced together that day is itself the story of a community 'gathered together and created' by the word of God:

> Israel BC was ... constituted, from one point of view, as the people who heard God's word – in call, promise, liberation, guidance, judgment, forgiveness, further judgment, renewed liberation and renewed promise ... scripture was never simply about the imparting of information ... The story was told in order to generate once more the sense of Israel as the people called by YHWH for his purposes in the world, so that the writing and the telling of the story formed the further living embodiment of YHWH's call and promise. It was written to shape and direct the life of God's people.[174]

The apostles continued to tell this ancient story, interpreting it now in the light of the life, death and resurrection of Jesus and discovering it to be

> God's own power, at work through the freshly outpoured Spirit, calling into being the new covenant people, the restored Israel-for-the-world … The church was thus from the very beginning characterized, precisely as the transformed people of God, as the community created by God's call and promise, and summoned to hear the 'word' of the gospel in all its fullness.[175]

The picture that the Bible itself paints for us of people's engagement with God's word is characteristically *communal* and *oral*. Old and New Testaments record that people normally listened *together* as a leader or priest proclaimed the word of God as they had received it, either in oral or written form. Response to the word tended to be communal – though not necessarily unanimous. This communal and oral engagement was the norm either because God's word was not yet preserved as text or because the writings regarded as God's word were only available in limited form, usually only to the priests and leaders of the people. Here are five examples of many others in Scripture:

- 'Then Moses went up to God; the Lord called to him from the mountain, saying, "Thus shall you say to the house of Jacob … These are the words that you shall speak to the Israelites." So Moses came, summoned the elders of the people, and set before them all these words that the Lord had commanded him. The people all answered as one: "Everything that the Lord has spoken we will do"' (Exod. 19:3–8).
- 'When the seventh month came – the people of Israel being settled in their towns – all the people gathered together into the square before the Water Gate. They told the scribe Ezra to bring the book of the law of Moses, which the Lord had given to Israel … Ezra … read from it … and the ears of all the people were attentive to the book of the law … the people wept when they heard the words of the law' (Neh. 7:73 – 8:9).
- 'When he came to Nazareth … [Jesus] went to the synagogue on the Sabbath day as was his custom. He stood up to read, and the scroll of the prophet Isaiah was given to him … The eyes of all in the synagogue were fixed on him. Then he began to say to them, "Today this scripture has been fulfilled in your hearing …"' (Luke 4:16–21).

- 'And when this letter has been read among you, have it read also in the church of the Laodiceans; and see that you read also the letter from Laodicea' (Col. 4:16).[176]
- 'Blessed is the one who reads aloud the words of the prophecy, and blessed are those who hear it and who keep what is written in it; for the time is near' (Rev. 1:3).

In oral cultures, memory is crucial. Words must be transmitted by repetition as well as by being preserved in written form. Moses urged his people to repeat God's words that he had transmitted to them, to communicate them to the next generation and to make them part of the fabric of their homes (Deut. 6:6–9). The poet of Psalm 119 describes a process of internalizing God's word so that it can continually do its work: 'I treasure your word in my heart, so that I may not sin against you' (Ps. 119:11).

When Paul urges Timothy to come to him quickly in Rome, and to bring with him 'the books, and above all the parchments' (2 Tim. 4:13), the Greek words he uses are *biblia* and *membrana*. The *biblia* would have been a collection of small scrolls, while the *membrana* were specially prepared animal skins. Some scholars have suggested that in this second word, Paul may have been referring to a very early form of book, a *codex* of *membrana* that were sewn together. *Codices* became popular among the early Christian communities because they made it easier to move back and forth in a document and to have more material collected into the same document – an entire Gospel, for example.[177] Paul's *biblia* and *membrana* were rare treasures, laboriously hand-written. The eager and receptive Beroean Jews whom Luke describes in Acts 17 would not have been sitting around with private copies of the scriptures. They were meeting for discussion in the synagogue and almost certainly reading and debating the scriptures contained in the synagogue's collection of scrolls (Acts 17:10, 11). Most members of the churches to whom Paul and the other apostles wrote would not have owned personal copies of Scripture documents. They would have depended largely on public reading of the texts – a practice that continued for the next fourteen centuries.

The privatizing of Scripture

Around 1439 came a momentous change in communications. In Germany Johannes Gutenberg adapted the screw press, used for cloth and grapes, to incorporate movable type so as to print text. The Gutenberg Bible in Latin was the first book ever printed. Mass production of any text, including the Bible, now became possible, 'an explosion of such overwhelming power that we continue to feel its reverberations today'.[178]

In his intriguing re-reading of Marshall McLuhan's communication theory, summarized in the famous phrase 'the medium is the message', Shane Hipps identifies significant ways in which the invention of printing has shaped the Christian church, especially in its engagement with the Bible. The first of these, he suggests, is that access to the Bible in print inevitably made people more *individualistic* in their interaction with God's word:

> As writing becomes the dominant communication system, people no longer need the community to retain teachings, traditions, or identity. As a result they spend greater amounts of time reflecting in private. This increased isolation creates a new emphasis on individualism … The modern age conceived of a gospel that matters primarily for the individual. The gospel was reduced to forgiveness as a transaction, a concern for personal morality, and the intellectual pursuit of doctrinal precision. In this view the Bible became little more than an individual's handbook for moral living and right thinking. As a result, printing had a tendency to erode the communal nature of faith. The church community became little more than a collection of discrete individuals working on their personal relationships with Jesus.[179]

In the Western church it is easy to see signs of this individualism. We can choose, according to our theological tradition, gender, age and occupation, from hundreds of different (especially English) versions of the Bible. We can underline or highlight those Bibles in ways that reflect our individual response to God's word. And as Conder and Rhodes point out,

> It is only a small jump … from 'my Bible' to inflexible and authoritarian interpretations … In many ways, we live in an era of rival, authoritarian proclamations about the message of the Bible. There is an abundance of loud voices telling us 'the final word' about the Word.[180]

Eugene Peterson similarly declares:

> Print is technology. We pick up a Bible and find that we have God's word in our hands, *our hands*. We can now handle it. It is easy enough

> to suppose that we are in control of it, that we can use it, that we are
> in charge of applying it wherever, whenever, and to whomever we
> wish without regard to appropriateness or conditions ... those who
> don't know the conditions implicit in the technology of the Bible are
> ... dangerous to themselves and others.[181]

Print technology – for all its wonders – can undermine our sense of being addressed by the God who speaks and commands us to listen. It removes the essentially *relational* quality of God's word, which, as we discovered in chapter 3, 'is a word that can rightly expect a response' (p. 30).

This shift away from listening to God together has also resulted for much of the church today in a loss of any expectation that God's word addresses us for a *purpose* – that of shaping us to be a community of people who live out God's kingdom ways of justice and peace and love. If we read Scripture at all, we read selectively for comfort, for information, to analyze and to control. We are inexperienced in what Peterson describes as *formative* Bible reading, 'A way of reading that intends the fusion of the entire biblical story and my story. A way of reading that ... *intends the living of the text.*'[182]

Before you read on, take some time to reflect on your own practices of engaging with the Bible. Are these mainly private and personal or mainly communal, or a good balance of both? How has your practice changed over time and why? If you are a church leader how are you currently encouraging your congregation to interact with the word of God? To what extent does God's word play a formative role in your own life and your church's life?

Returning the Bible to the community

For Dietrich Bonhöffer to start to read Scripture with the intention of *living* it was a conversion moment. This young Lutheran pastor was a key figure in the Confessing Church that stood against the Nazis in Germany. In a letter to his fiancée in 1936 he described his disturbing discovery that although he preached and was deeply involved in church life, *he was not a Christian.* He had come to understand that he had always read the Bible *for* himself and that he needed to start to read it *over-against* himself. In particular, he re-read the Sermon on the Mount over-against himself and experienced it as a great liberation. In 1935 he took charge of an 'underground' seminary recently founded by the Confessing Church in Finkenwalde. Here he developed an ethos that he described as 'common life under the Word'.[183] For him, community was the only adequate context in which to learn to engage with God's word wisely and turn that engagement into Christian living in the world. But he also understood clearly that reading Scripture together did not *automatically* mean that a community would live out God's purposes in the world. In Germany the wider church was reading Scripture and responding to it in very different ways from the Confessing Church. The difference lay in whether the community submitted Scripture to the claims of humanity's values and views or submitted humanity's values and views to the claims of Scripture. Bonhöffer had understood that:

> the presentation of the gospel is best achieved not through methodological principles or through the attempt to make Scripture 'relevant'. It is achieved when people are willing to allow the present age in general, and our lives in particular, to be interrogated by the Scriptures. The German Christians only read the Bible *for* themselves, discarding what they didn't want. But the call is to read Scripture *over-against* ourselves, allowing Scripture to question our lives.[184]

We have seen elsewhere in this book other examples of how a Scripture-reading community can be more – or less – faithful to the direction of God's word. Beyers Naudé's church community believed they had constructed a Scripture-based theology of apartheid. It was only when he moved into a wider community and encountered the pastoral problems caused by that apartheid theology that he began to read Scripture 'over-against' himself and his theological community – and was changed for ever. The same happened in the case of David Bruce, reading Scripture in the context of a sectarian Protestant community in Ireland and then, because of the tragedy of his friend's murder, starting to read the New Testament 'over-against' himself and to build bridges with the Catholic community. The Jewish community of Jesus' day was one that tended to read the Hebrew Scriptures 'for' itself, blind to any understanding other than its own, opposed to any 'over-against' reading (Mark 12:10; John 5:39, 40). The disappointed disciples on the Emmaus road needed to hear Jesus' 'over-against' reading of their Scriptures, one that turned upside down the narrowly self-interested understandings that they had inherited (Luke 24:25–27).

In the Western church, as well as a general privatizing of Scripture and a refusal to read it 'over-against' ourselves, we face a situation of catastrophic biblical illiteracy. In the UK the year 2011 will mark the 400th anniversary of the King James' Bible. But a research project by St John's College in Durham reveals that 60% of people surveyed had no idea who the Good Samaritan was and 57% knew nothing of the story of Joseph. A confirmation class of six people could name between them only nine books of the Bible. Of course even when people have extensive knowledge of the Bible's content it doesn't by any means guarantee that they are engaging with that content in ways that bring about transformation. Maybe this widespread lack of knowledge, especially in Western cultures, can make it possible for God's word to take people by surprise, astonishing them by the connections they suddenly perceive between Scripture and their lives. We saw that process at work in the stories of Nurat and others in chapter 1. However, the situation of ignorance of the Bible story presents us with major challenges. Henri Bacher, reflecting on the situation in France, talks about the total disconnection of his compatriots from their Judaeo-Christian roots:

> Belief in the widest sense of the word has not disappeared, but explicit references to Christianity have been binned. It is not unusual for children or adults visiting a museum to have no idea who this 'chick' holding her 'kid' is, or why they appear in so many paintings … For several centuries, the majority of native Europeans were catechised … Movements seeking to spread and popularise the Bible could therefore count on certain givens that made it much easier to understand the Bible text. It was like seeds planted by others which, when they come into contact with water, bud and blossom … When addressing new converts, the evangelist was drawing on a legacy of knowledge that was just waiting to come to life. Today the same message gets lost, finding no anchoring point. It's like a climber who finds himself up against a smooth rock face, without any grips.[185]

What steps might we take then to seek to turn the tide of indifference and ignorance about the Bible and to engage people in the kind of formative communal interaction with Scripture that reads God's word over-against itself in the expectation of living it out? One thing is certain: there is no magic 'silver bullet' approach to the kind of Scripture engagement that brings about fruitful change in individuals and communities. No single package or programme or approach is guaranteed success. The ideas that we explore in the rest of this chapter are suggestions that have been tested but all of them will need to be reshaped for different contexts.

Teaching

The Catholic Church has taken very seriously the mandate of the second Vatican Council. The Dogmatic Constitution on Divine Revelation, *Dei Verbum,* stated that 'Easy access to Sacred Scripture should be provided for all the Christian faithful' and 'earnestly and especially urges all the Christian faithful, especially Religious, to learn by frequent reading of the divine Scriptures the "excellent knowledge of Jesus Christ" (Phil. 3:8). "For ignorance of the Scriptures is ignorance of Christ."'[186] Workshops of the kind described at the beginning of this chapter are typical of a wide range of learning opportunities for the laity, equipping them with tools to navigate the Bible and explore its implications without being snared in fundamentalist readings.

Depending on the local needs, which will require research and adequate listening processes, any church that gives priority to enabling people to engage with God's word should consider providing creative learning opportunities to help people to understand:

- how the Bible came to exist and why we can have confidence in the quality of Bible manuscripts
- how the Bible fits together and tells a coherent story (as in the workshop described at the start of this chapter)
- common-sense interpretational principles that take into account the Bible author's intentions, the kinds of literature the Bible contains, and the contemporary context and significance.

The word 'creative' is important! The church needs to take seriously the fact that people learn in different ways, and adapt its approaches accordingly. When I first moved back to Scotland, I started to go to a local church and eventually discussed membership with the minister. He told me that anyone joining the church had to attend an Alpha course. Rather reluctantly I signed on and found the first session to be very different from what I'd experienced at my church in London! We didn't start with a meal together, just broke for tea and a biscuit at half time, and it was more of a formal lecture than a free-flowing discussion. In fact no one said anything, even when questions and comments were invited. But the second session, on the person of Jesus, was quite different. Instead of standing up and delivering a lecture, the minister told us that he had brought with him his collection of images of Jesus – classical and modern paintings and drawings and photos of great art such as Michelangelo's *Pietà*. 'I'm going to spread them out on the table, and I'd like you all to have a look at them and choose the one that means most to you and then tell the rest of the group why you chose that particular picture.' I waited for the usual silence. But this time people moved quickly to the table and were soon making their choice and eagerly telling the group why they had chosen this particular picture of Jesus. The link was always to something in their life that they related to this particular representation of Jesus: on the cross, talking to the woman at the Samaritan well, healing Peter's mother-in-law, calling Zacchaeus down from the tree. The ice was well and truly broken because the minister had somehow sensed that this group would remain tongue-tied as long as he insisted that they interact with the written text of the Bible. Relating to image rather than text released them to talk, both about their lives and about the Jesus they had come to know.

In chapter 7 we discussed Bible engagement with children and young people. There needs to be a continuum between our Bible engagement approaches with the younger generation and with adults. Engaging with God's word with adults often becomes too focused on analytical, propositional thinking and ignores the intuitive and imaginative aspects of the person. It's worth remembering that Glenn Cupit emphasizes that none of the 'rungs' on the child's ladder of meaning ever becomes irrelevant for us as adults. We *add* implication and context to the earlier enjoyment, emotion and imagination that enabled us to attribute meaning to any aspect of life. We don't *replace* the earlier ways of exploring meaning (see p. 108).

N. T. Wright advocates Scripture engagement that is 'refreshed by appropriate scholarship'.[187] This is an important aspect of teaching the Bible in the community of the church. There needs to be a lively interaction between the community of the church and the community of Christian scholars. Too often vitally helpful research never leaves the confines of the academy because it is expressed in language and concepts that most ordinary people struggle with. It is encouraging to find the important ideas contained in a monumental work such as Richard Bauckham's *Jesus and the Eyewitnesses* made available in a more accessible form as *The Gospels as Eyewitness Testimony*.[188] Once again, we have much to learn from the Catholics here, both in their determination not to make people overly dependent on 'experts' and in their realism about the need to provide people with the tools to enable them to explore Scripture and interpret it in healthy and helpful ways.

Preaching

In many churches around the world the sermon is the only way in which people can engage with Scripture. It is a minority of churches, especially Protestant churches, that provide people with opportunities like those described in the section above to learn, for example, to engage wisely with Scripture in order to grow as disciples of Jesus Christ. Preaching therefore offers a significant opportunity to commend God's word to people and build their confidence in its trustworthiness and significance for their lives. We recall Thielicke's damning criticism of sermons that amount to 'Christian gobbledegook that never gets under anybody's skin' (p. 22). Preaching must go beyond exegesis of the text, however skilled and scholarly, to open up the implications for our lives today. I remember once taking a friend to a church renowned for its evangelistic preaching. She was starting to explore Christianity and I hoped and prayed that the sermon that evening on Romans 8 ('There is therefore now no condemnation') might speak specifically to her needs. We heard a brilliant dissection of the text, an exposition of the highest order. But at the end of it, we both knew that our question was, 'So what?' In response to this malaise, Eugene Peterson calls for a return to what he calls 'contemplative exegesis', a different style of preaching that takes seriously the *oral* and *narrative* nature of Scripture:

> Words are sounds that reveal. Words make stories that shape. Contemplative exegesis means opening our interiors to these revealing sounds and submitting our lives to the story these words tell in order to be shaped by them.[189]

Oral / aural approaches

Even in the so-called developed world, there are thousands of people who struggle to engage with text and are, by preference, oral and visual learners and communicators. Different models of ministry are being developed to meet their needs. One example is a group called Unlock that works with people in areas of urban deprivation in the UK, people for whom an inductive-style analysis of a text would be completely foreign. Unlock has developed models for working with the Bible in non-book cultures. Like the Catholic base communities, they take people's life situations as the starting point and move from them to encourage dialogue with the Bible text in expectation that Scripture will address people's life issues.[190]

Another important aspect of oral/aural Bible engagement is the public reading of Scripture. In many churches today this is almost non-existent. Preachers often refer to one or two verses of the Bible and the community has little sense, if any, of an unfolding, coherent narrative. Even in those churches where the lectionary texts are a central aspect of the service, the reading is rarely done in such a way that it grips the hearers and draws them in. Why not offer workshops in the public reading of the Bible? Every reading is an interpretation; people could be drawn into discussion together about the meaning of the text and how it can most helpfully be proclaimed in public.

Why not gather a group of friends to take turns reading aloud a chosen passage, experimenting with how different emphases and tones of voice can communicate the passage in different ways? Can you agree on a 'right' way of reading the passage or do you discover that there may be several 'right' ways?

Digital Bible engagement

In 2006 CELAM, the Latin American Episcopal Conference, working with the United Bible Societies in the Americas and with CEBIPAL, the Biblical Pastoral Centre for Latin America, embarked on a most interesting experiment in Bible engagement. Called *Lectionautas*, it combines the centuries-old practice of *Lectio Divina*, prayerful meditation on the Bible text, with the most contemporary of media – an interactive website and short videos posted on YouTube in which groups of young 'lectionauts' share their discoveries in the Bible. The introduction to the manual that this programme uses to equip young people to practise *Lectio Divina* sets out three pieces of essential 'navigational equipment': an open heart, a desire to know more about Jesus, and the joy and creativity that characterize many young people. It tells these adolescents that in joining *Lectionautas* they will be getting to know new brothers and sisters that God gives them, because this will not be an individual, solitary experience, but a journey of friends who, like Jesus' friends, will form a community.[191] Each day, the website provides young people with the Bible text in dramatized audio format. For each Sunday, special resources are provided to help individuals or groups to reflect on the lectionary readings that will be preached on. The *Lectio Divina* process starts with prayer to the Holy Spirit, then the repeated reading of (or listening to) the Bible text, meditation on the text, prayer arising out of interaction with the word, and finally contemplation, which is explained as seeing with the eyes of God the whole of life so that we ask ourselves, 'What is God showing me (us) what I (we) should do?' A parallel website, www.discipulitos.com provides similar material for younger children.

This model encourages engagement with the Bible both on an individual level and in the context of a small group, in preparation for hearing the word of God within the church community on Sunday. This multi-directional reinforcement is very powerful. The concept of reinforcement is also at the heart of the E100 project from Scripture Union in the USA. One hundred 'essential' Bible passages take people through the entire Bible story from Genesis to Revelation. They can read these as individuals or engage with group resources – preferably both. Sermon outlines are also available. As the New Zealand E100 website asks, 'Imagine what could happen if tens of thousands of Kiwi Christians are reading the Bible together.'[192] In Australia and New Zealand the project draws together the national Bible Societies, Wycliffe Bible Translators and Scripture Union and uses a range of social networking sites (Facebook, YouTube, Twitter and mobile phone applications) to reinforce people's experience of interacting with Scripture in a wide community.

However we also need to hear Henri Bacher warning us against thinking that digital Bible engagement will miraculously solve the problems of indifference to the Bible:

> Book-based civilisation has locked the word into texts and speeches; electronic orality is going to follow the same path, packaging the word into emotional parcels made up of image and sound bites. As Christians we must learn once more to work on the word in order to communicate. God does not write and neither does he show himself. He *speaks* … Before adopting the culture of books or of electronic orality, Christians should be at ease in their own culture, in the ways that people of that culture speak and speak to each other, and that God speaks to them. It is only in community, in the widest sense of that word, that we can speak to each other.[193]

The Bible and the arts

Many churches and para-church groups encourage Bible quizzes and competitions that focus on Bible knowledge. As we reflected earlier in this chapter, while knowledge of the Bible's contents is an important aspect of engagement, even more important is the internalization of the word, true engagement with it. Events that focus on Scripture memorization and the public reciting of Scripture are more important than information-based activities. Mark's Gospel has often made a significant impact as a theatre production:

> 'More than any other Gospel, Mark lends itself to theatre,' says Jeffrey Fiske, who also directed *The Screwtape Letters*. 'It is written as if a reporter is sending first hand reports of Jesus' remarkable journey from rural obscurity to urban sensation to political assassination. The dialogue is both compelling and funny. Max McLean humanizes what are often seen by secular society as distant archetypes. He plays each character as a real human being, sometimes rendered comical in gape-mouthed incredulity by the miracles of a man who warns them "not to tell anyone". That, of course, is the very thing they do.'[194]

We have referred earlier in this chapter to the way that image can unlock the process of engagement with the Bible that text is often powerless to do. In the year 2000, to mark the millennium, an exhibition called 'Seeing Salvation' opened at the National Gallery in London. Thousands of people moved through seven galleries of paintings, drawings and sculpture depicting the life and death of Jesus. The director of the Gallery, Neil McGregor, received many more letters and emails than usual about the exhibition and he turned them over to Professor Grace Davie, a specialist in the sociology of religion, for analysis:

> The refrain Davie detects through the *Seeing Salvation* correspondence reminds us of the need for the church to have cultural courage and to access the riches of its inheritance. If and when it does this, it can touch people deeply and inspire them to get active. The National Gallery was overrun with visitors by the end of the exhibition. A chord was struck and people responded.[195]

Music is another significant arena in which people can be brought together in interaction with God's word through a medium that may be important to them. I recently went to a church service at which the words of Allegri's *Miserere*, translated into English, were projected on to a screen as we listened to the choir sing this beautiful version of David's prayer of repentance (Ps. 51). This led into a simple conversational reflection on the theme of penitence and forgiveness, and then a communion service. Many of the mostly young congregation were clearly deeply moved, staying on after the service for personal prayer or to talk with the leaders.

Drama, music, image: these are all deeply contextualized art forms. A European seventeenth century version of Psalm 51 will not necessarily resonate in an African context. As in the case of all the models of Bible engagement that we have considered in this chapter and others, we must listen to our context in all its dimensions and provide means of exploring God's word that speak in that context.

It is easy to become discouraged today in the face of secular hostility to the Bible, of indifference within much of the church in the West and of fundamentalist hijacking of Scripture. But as Paul writes to the Christians in Rome,

> Whatever was written ahead of time ... was written for us to learn from, so that through patience, and through the encouragement of the Bible, we might have hope (Rom. 15:4, Tom Wright's translation).[196]

God's Spirit is a creative Spirit who works through people like Sister Teresa with whom this chapter began, hopeful and faithful people who are passionately committed to enabling others to hear and respond to God's life-giving word.

9

Living Word

The Word was God ... and
... became flesh and lived among us
— John 1:1, 14

One way of thinking about the Gospels is as four records of how Jesus, the incarnate Word of God, engaged with the Scriptures of his people, the word of God that told a story that was ultimately about himself. Matthew, Mark, Luke and John provide us with four intriguing accounts of how Jesus understood and engaged with the Hebrew Scriptures and encouraged others to do, as he preached and taught, meditated privately, debated in public worship and encouraged individuals and groups of people to make connections between God's word and their lives. This chapter will explore what models and guidelines we may find in these accounts that might shape both how we interact with the Bible and encourage others to do so.

By the time Jesus started his public ministry, his mind and heart were steeped in the Jewish Scriptures. The Gospels don't record how this happened, how Jesus learned to read and write, to reason and reflect on life and the Scriptures of his people. But it's clear that such a process did take place, in part surely through the normal cycle of Jewish family life with its celebrations and commemorations and their corresponding Scriptures and prayers, and probably also in the Nazareth synagogue school, the Bet has-Sefer or 'School of the Book' which existed in every town and village in Palestine, thanks to the efforts of the Pharisees. Luke gives us a tantalizing glimpse of the twelve-year old Jesus in the Jerusalem temple, listening to the rabbis, asking and responding to questions, astounding his elders by the quality of his understanding (Luke 2:45–47). For the next eighteen years or so (Luke 3:23), public and private reflection on the Scriptures must surely have been part of the process through which 'Jesus increased in wisdom … and in divine and human favour' (Luke 2:52) as he grew up alongside his brothers and sisters and experienced the normal disciplines of that Nazareth home (Luke 2:51).

The Gospels record Jesus' quotations from, and allusions to, some twenty-four of the books of the Old Testament. He generally used the collective term 'the scriptures' or 'scripture' (Matt 26:54, John 5:39, Luke 4:21) or referred to one or more of the traditional divisions of the Hebrew canon: the Law, the Prophets and the Writings (Luke 16:16, 24:44, Matt. 11:13). Jesus often shaped his teaching by referring to a range of different Scriptures. The opening section of Luke's account of the Sermon on the Mount (Luke 6:20–26), for example, echoes in its four blessings and four woes the Deuteronomy lists of blessings and curses (Deut. 27:11 – 28:1–6). But Jesus' listeners would also have recognized allusions to Isaiah, Jeremiah, Amos, Micah and several psalms in his words about the poor, the hungry, the rich, the false prophets and those who grieve. Jesus rarely quoted Scripture in an isolated, 'proof text' kind of way. Rather it is as if these writings had become part of the air he breathed, or a deep well from which to draw resources to reflect on and evaluate any situation he encountered. In the book of Revelation we find something similar in the way in which John the Evangelist draws on the Scriptures. In the book's 404 verses there are 518 references to the Hebrew Scriptures but not a single direct quotation. The implication is that

> though St. John is immersed in scripture and submits himself to it, he does not merely repeat it – it is recreated in him. He does not quote scripture in order to prove something; rather he assimilates scripture so that he becomes someone.[197]

Jesus explored his identity and calling through Scripture

We can sometimes pay lip service to aspects of Christian doctrine without ever really entering into the implications of our beliefs. This kind of disconnection can come to light when we're exploring the Bible. I remember an experience with a group in my church in La Paz, Bolivia. We were reading Matthew's account of Jesus calming the storm (Matt. 8:23–27). As we reflected on why Jesus could sleep the middle of a storm, it became clear that almost everyone in the group believed that he did so to test his disciples' faith. But what did this mean in terms of Jesus' trustworthiness? Did we really want to follow a Jesus who faked sleep in order to test his followers? Exploring the wider context of the passage enabled people to begin to accept that perhaps Jesus took the opportunity to rest simply because he was exhausted after days of non-stop activity. His sleep was a normal human response. Everyone in that group subscribed to the orthodox doctrine of the divinity and humanity of Jesus. But when it came to interpreting this specific text and thinking through its implications for our own discipleship, people found it difficult to hold together the paradoxical truth about Jesus' identity as fully human and fully divine.

When we meditate on the human and divine character of Jesus we may wonder how Scripture informed his own understanding of his identity and mission. By what process did he 'find himself' in the Scriptures? It must have begun in Jesus' childhood as Luke makes clear at the start of his Gospel in the touching snatch of dialogue between Mary and her son: 'Child, why have you treated us like this? Look, your father and I have been searching for you in great anxiety... Why were you searching for me? Did you not know that I must be in my Father's house?' (Luke 2:48, 49).

And was another turning point for Jesus' self-understanding his baptism? He hears God address him in terms that echo the Hebrew Scriptures, 'This is my Son, the Beloved, with whom I am well pleased' (Matt. 3:17). At least two Old Testament texts echo in this affirmation that proclaims Jesus as Son of God and Messiah (Ps. 2:2, 7) and his Beloved one (Isa. 42:1). Isaiah is speaking here of the 'servant' whose suffering will mysteriously restore the relationship between God and his people (Isa. 40–55). There may also be an echo here of God's words to Abraham, 'Take your son, your only son...whom you love' (Gen. 22:2). During those days in the desert following his baptism, as well as countering with God's word the devil's attacks on his identity ('If you are the Son of God...', Matt. 4:3, 6), was Jesus also meditating on the implications of his Father's affirmation as a call also to suffering and self-giving?

God's word is also our primary resource for knowing who we are and why we exist. As Jesus did throughout his life, we can explore in Scripture the implications both of being God's beloved sons and daughters (1 John 4:10) and of responding to that love (Matt. 16:24–26). But the Bible is not a blueprint or an instruction manual to be followed mechanically. Rather it is a story or a drama that invites our participation. We introduced this idea in chapter 4 (p. 56) when we described the Bible story as a drama in six acts:

- Act 1   Creation
- Act 2   The Fall
- Act 3   The story of Israel
- Act 4   The story of Jesus
- Act 5   The story of the church
- Act 6   New creation

N. T. Wright has developed this idea further by suggesting that we can understand our lives as a participation in the fifth act, the story of the church. Within this act we live in an in-between time – after the apostolic period but not yet in the new creation of Act 6 of the biblical drama, described in passages such as 1 Corinthians 15 or Revelation 21 and 22. We could describe our lives as developing our chapter in the story or improvising our part in the drama. But 'our' chapter or 'our' part needs to fit and be coherent with the acts that have already been provided for us in the Bible and also be shaped by the promise of the wonderfully hopeful final act:

> We must act in the appropriate manner for *this* moment in the story;
> this will be in direct continuity with the previous acts (we are not free
> to jump suddenly to another narrative, a different play altogether),
> but such continuity also implies discontinuity, a moment where
> genuinely new things can and do happen.[198]

Understanding the *discontinuities* with the earlier acts of the Bible drama can help us with a question we raised in chapter 3 when we were exploring the authority of the Bible and realized that as God's people today we don't practise animal sacrifice or stone our rebellious sons to death (p. 33). 'We are not members of Israel BC; so – as one example out of many – we ought not to rebuild the Jerusalem Temple and offer animal sacrifices in it.'[199]

It can be helpful to keep in mind this idea of Scripture as a drama as we watch and listen to Jesus interacting with the word of his Father. He does not have a detailed script in front of him, telling him what to do and say next. There is nothing mechanical about his understanding of, and living out of Scripture. In his humanity he is, like us, feeling his way as he works out what it means to live God's word. For example, all three synoptic Gospels describe Jesus' refusal to promise an easy life to his followers; following him will involve carrying a cross (Matt. 10:38; Mark 8:34; Luke 9:23). Jesus is apparently aware (through his meditations on passages such as Isaiah 53?) that his mission involves terrible suffering. But the same Gospels also record his struggle to accept from his Father the 'cup' of suffering involved in the cross and all it implied (Matt. 26:39, 42; Mark 14:36; Luke 22:42).

Jesus' engagement with Scripture moves him to compassion and to anger

Perhaps some of the texts that Jesus pondered most deeply were those that dealt with the true and false shepherds of Israel. God's grieving word through Ezekiel to the nation's leaders, 'You have not strengthened the weak, you have not healed the sick ... you have not sought the lost, but with force and harshness you have ruled them' (Ezek. 34:4) resonates at many points in the Gospels and especially in Jesus' claim to be the good shepherd (John 10:11). Matthew and Mark describe Jesus' attitude to the crowds as that of a compassionate shepherd who sees, not a mass of anonymous faces but 'harassed and helpless ... sheep without a shepherd' (Matt. 9:36, Mark 6:34). It is the response of a true shepherd that prompts Jesus' anger at the callous legalists for whom scripture is a weapon of control, and moves him to heal their victim (Matt. 12:9–13). It is a compassionate and angry pastor who challenges the religious leaders to self-examination and launches a guilty woman on a new way of life by pronouncing 'no condemnation' (John 8:2–11).

Jesus always noticed those whom others would overlook or despise. They were of great significance to him – the timid widow offering her last coins (Luke 21:2), the wealthy but despised tax collector (Luke 19:1–7), the Roman soldier who cared for his servant (Matt. 8:5–10).

We have so much to learn from this Jesus, the compassionate and sometimes angry shepherd, both in our own engagement with Scripture and in our encouragement of others to do so. A simple way to start would be to ask ourselves how we see those among whom we live and serve. Are we 'moved by compassion' as we look out over our congregation, our house group, our colleagues at work, the young people we teach, that sea of faces at rush hour, the people in the headlines today, those hurrying past us in the street or crowded into the bus or train?

Jesus challenged the dominant understandings of Scripture

As we have seen, Jesus the good shepherd habitually challenged those readings of Scripture that had become oppressive, part of the armoury of a dominant group in society. How easily a sacred text – even the Bible –

can become a tool for the exercise of power, when we start to give priority to our own agendas, our own emphases, our own interests, as so many of the community leaders did in Jesus' time. Carlos Mesters, writing of his experiences of reading Scripture with poor communities in Brazil, recounts:

> A priest said to me, 'When I read or hear some interpretations of the Bible, I get the impression that people have a hidden agenda. Before starting to interpret the text, they know what they're going to find in it. They reduce the meaning of the Bible to the scale of their own ideas.' And another added: 'It's an ideological, tendentious, use of the Bible.'[200]

Jesus fiercely denounces those who have taken God's word in the Mosaic law and turned it into a tool to dominate others, while themselves disregarding the rules. 'They tie up heavy burdens, hard to bear, and lay them on the shoulders of others; but they themselves are unwilling to lift a finger to move them' (Matt. 23:4). N. T. Wright warns against reading this only as a denunciation of behaviour in the religious establishment:

> The scribes and Pharisees were not simply what we would call 'religious' leaders. They were, just as much, what we would call social and political leaders, or at least the leaders of popular parties and pressure groups ... Before we indulge, as Christians, in inward-looking polemic against other members of our own family of faith, let's be clear that the problem Jesus identified is not confined to churches, but runs through most modern societies from top to bottom.[201]

I think of a sad email that arrived received recently from a discouraged young leader in East Asia:

> Yes, I'm feeling stressed. There are a lot of things that I couldn't put in the last email. I was having dinner with some board members and guests, when the wife of one board member (who attends the same church as me) openly criticized me regarding a certain political issue in my church as well as making clear that she was not happy that I'm dating a girl from another church (one that she obviously had some personal opinions about). To make matters worse, none of the other board members seemed to be really bothered to stop her.

I felt deeply humiliated in front of our guests, many of whom are teachers who I am ministering to.[202]

Jesus challenges attitudes of expertise in matters of faith and Scripture

Jesus' profound and wide-ranging interaction with the Scriptures and with matters of faith was always exercised with great humility as well as with extraordinary authority. We can see this at work in all kinds of ways. Jesus engages in theological, scriptural discourse with a solitary woman at Jacob's well near Sychar (John 4:5–26). He made all kinds of people feel valued and worth listening to, not only those who could talk theology professionally!

Jesus' attitude to, and sayings about, children, make it clear that he understood that the vulnerable humility of a child or the person open to being childlike was the most fruitful soil for the subversive, life-changing teaching of God's kingdom (Matt. 18:3, 4). One of Jesus' moments of greatest joy came with the realization of the mysterious ways in which his Father was determined to work – even through the incongruous band of followers whose most important credential was not their power over demons but their enrolment in God's purposes: 'You have hidden these things from the wise and intelligent and have revealed them to infants' (Luke 10:21).

How can we work out this kind of attitude in our lives and ministries? Are we tempted to write some people off as unlikely to contribute anything to our understanding of the Bible, to the life of our church, community or work situation? Are we alert to the insights that can come through the children and young people we relate to? Do we deliberately make space for more timid people to make a contribution? Do we value those who do the less high-profile tasks? Do we give too much importance to those who are educated, literate and articulate? Do we ever spend meaningful time with those on the margins of society?

Jesus' authority was rooted in his living and teaching of Scripture

By this time it's possible that you are wondering how all this can be related to the question of Jesus' interaction with Scripture. We haven't gone into many details on his hermeneutical practice or how he read specific Old Testament books. This is true. But it seems important to make the case for the inextricable weaving together of Jesus' understanding and teaching of Scripture with the way he lived and moved and had his being – especially his relationships with people and the range of people with whom he related. This interweaving is directly related to the authority which people perceived in Jesus' teaching and preaching. Put simply, Jesus *did* what he *said*, his life and his teaching were one integrated whole, unlike many of his contemporary religious professionals, who, as we have seen, were hypocrites, adept at telling others what to do and upholding those traditions convenient to them while sliding out of their responsibilities themselves (Matt. 15:1–7). This was what the Roman centurion admired in him, as we saw in Chapter 3 (pp. 30–31). This integrity was what so astounded the Capernaum crowds (Mark 1:22, 27).

Jesus didn't give his disciples lessons in techniques of evangelism or healing or dealing with unclean spirits. No, he *formed* them, 'made' them into fishers of people, taking them on the road with him, opening his lodgings and his life up to them, encouraging their questions, dealing with their doubts, showing them what integrity of word and action looked like, and then trusting them in new and challenging situations.

This coherence of teaching and life is absolutely central to the issues of effective Scripture engagement. As Bishop David Zac Niringiye has written,

> The life of anyone who belongs to Jesus is not about ministry; it's about *following*. I am not 'in ministry'. I am following Jesus. My primary definition of who I am is not ministry; I'm a follower of Jesus. That's it! I therefore think that we need to move away from a major paradigm within evangelical thinking, away from the Great Commission to the Great Invitation. Away from the Great Commission – sent to do things – to the Great Invitation to follow Jesus wherever he goes.[203]

The first of the 'Key Factors' that the Scripture Engagement Group of the Forum of Bible Agencies International has proposed is this:

> Transformational Scripture engagement may be strengthened by being constantly open and responsive ourselves to God's Word. Scripture engagement is not something we 'professionalize' and do to other people, but a process of mutuality in which we are all life-long learners.[204]

It is encouraging to hear news of Bible projects in which different Christian agencies and churches have committed themselves to collaboration – sometimes even giving up the publication of their names and logos – in response to Jesus' new commandment to love one another, which will be such a powerful witness to others (John 13:34, 35). KidsGames and Max7 are two such collaborative Bible engagement projects (see p. 144).

There is a further important aspect to the nature of the authority that people perceived in Jesus. They recognized that unlike the traditional religious interpreters of Scripture, Jesus was not a derivative thinker. There was something fresh and original about his readings of the ancient texts. This is especially notable about the teachings of the Sermon on the Mount in Matthew's Gospel.

> In the Sermon on the Mount Jesus is quite blunt: this, he says, is what
> *I* say to you. Never mind what you've heard from elsewhere. Never
> mind that the text has been read differently for over a thousand
> years. This is the way we have to read it now.[205]

Of course, we need to be cautious about what Jesus' example might imply for us today. This is not newness for its own sake. Jesus' re-readings of Scripture took people beyond a kind of routine acknowledgement of certain ethical demands ('You shall not murder', 'You shall not commit adultery') to an exploration of deeper and demanding implications and motivations.

Jesus' ministry was wholly dependent on the Holy Spirit

Jesus, John tells us, 'knew all people and needed no one to testify about anyone; for he himself knew what was in everyone' (John 2:24, 25). Time and again we watch Jesus discern a person's inward thoughts and needs and address the specific issues. Simon, the Pharisee host, silently disgusted at Jesus' willingness to be touched by a prostitute, finds Jesus reading his thoughts and drawing him reluctantly into a dialogue about forgiveness (Luke 7:36–50). The Samaritan woman is astonished at Jesus' discernment of her marital situation and the nature of her true need (John 4:16–26). The initially cynical Nathanael ('Can anything good come out of Nazareth?') experiences Jesus' profound understanding of him and is moved to worship (John 1:45–49). Discernment is one aspect of the Holy Spirit's work. Peter would later testify, 'You know … how God anointed Jesus of Nazareth with the Holy Spirit and with power; how he went about doing good and healing all who were oppressed by the devil, for God was with him' (Acts 10:36, 38).

On the night before his death, Jesus promises his disciples 'another Advocate, to be with you for ever ... the Holy Spirit, whom the Father will send in my name, will teach you everything ... He will glorify me' (John 14:16, 26; 16:14). So the discernment, the power, the compassion of Jesus are also to be characteristics of his followers as they seek to be faithful to him.

Jesus' life of prayer, interwoven with his reflection on Scripture, is a crucial aspect of his dependence on the Spirit. He understands and teaches the importance of persevering prayer (Luke 11:5–13) and seeks the spiritual resources he needs for his public ministry in solitude and prayer (Mark 1:35; Matt. 14:23; Luke 9:18).

In his use of Scripture, Jesus draws on old and new – relating ancient Scriptures to current life situations

Matthew's Gospel includes a brief passage, unique to his story of Jesus, about how 'every scribe who has been trained for the kingdom of heaven is like the master of a household who brings out of his treasure what is new and what is old' (Matt. 13:52). N. T. Wright suggests that Matthew may be hinting here that this is how he sees himself, combining in his account of Jesus' life the many references from, and allusions to, the ancient Jewish scriptures and especially the Mosaic teaching with Jesus' refreshing new parables and the startling evidence for the breaking in of the kingdom of God in healings and liberation from spiritual oppression.

The combination of old and new characterizes much of what Jesus did and taught. He was happy to proclaim the good news of the kingdom in the traditional places – the synagogues and the Jerusalem temple (Mark 6:2; Luke 4:16; Luke 19:47 etc). But he also met with people in unconventional settings, wherever they happened to be – in the fields, on the road, at home, by the lake (Matt. 13:1; Mark 2:1, 2; Luke 14:25).

Jesus offers little encouragement to us if we are seeking some kind of guaranteed formula in our approach to ministry, a method or a product that can be replicated in every situation. As we watch and listen to Jesus it becomes clear that he had no 'method' or standard approach. Each encounter is different, each reference to Scripture is there for a different reason. Often Jesus doesn't draw directly on Scripture at all, but tells a parable. The only unfailing constants are Jesus' discerning compassion for people, his refusal to coerce or manipulate anyone and the authority that derives from his own obedience to his Father's word.

What aspects of the ways in which Jesus engages with Scripture do you believe are most important, and why? Note down some words that you would use to describe how he goes about it. Which are the ones in which you believe you most need to grow?

At the close of this chapter and this book, I find myself reflecting once again on the way Jesus explained his own story, 'the things about himself in all the scriptures' to the two disciples on the Emmaus road. I wonder if he could have done this *before* his resurrection. Or did the pieces of the jigsaw, the story the Scriptures told about him, only finally fall into place for him in the new reality that came into being that Easter morning? And if so, is there encouragement here to us to continue to walk by faith and in reliance on God's Holy Spirit, as we work out, as we 'improvise' our lives in response to the story of God that we will only understand in its entirety on that day when we know fully and see face to face (1 Cor. 13:12). Meanwhile …

> the Author of the biblical drama has sent his Spirit to be our compassionate and empowering dramatic Director and Acting Coach, who helps us to discern what would be faithful improvisation in our own time. And recognizing that such historical-cultural improvisation is a fearful, anxiety-producing matter, God sends the Spirit precisely as a Comforter.[206]

Appendix 1

Additional Resources

Resources listed here are not mentioned elsewhere in the notes to chapters. The Forum of Bible Agencies International website has been mentioned but is highlighted here again as an important resource, especially if you join the 'Community' on the Scripture Engagement page.

Chapter 1. Transforming Word

Stories and testimonies of the impact of the Bible can be found on websites such as:

http://www.wycliffe.ca/transform/index.html

http://www.forum-intl.net/bible_cause/default.aspx?id=84

Chapter 3. God's Word

There is helpful and interesting information about how the Bible came into existence on:

http://www.biblesociety.org.uk/about-the-bible/history-of-the-bible

Gordon D. Fee and Douglas Stuart, *How to Read the Bible for All Its Worth* (Bletchley: Scripture Union, 1993) has helpful material on continuity and discontinuity between the Old and New Testaments. See particularly pp. 149–164.

Colin Sinclair, *The Hitch-Hiker's Guide to the Bible: Thumbing Through the Old and New Testament* (Oxford: Monarch Books, 2008) is a helpful and accessible guide to all the books of the Bible and their main themes.

Chapter 5. Offensive Word

Terry Brown (ed.), *Other Voices, Other Worlds: The Global Church Speaks Out On Homosexuality*, (London: Darton, Longman and Todd, 2006) offers insights on this issue from a wide range of cultures.

Chapter 6. Unique Word

A range of helpful resources on Islam and the Bible can be found on

http://www.cmcsoxford.org.uk/home.php?home=yes

Chapter 7. Young Word

Terry Clutterham and John Stephenson, *Top Tips on Exploring the Bible with Young People*, Bletchley: Scripture Union, 2009.

Terry Clutterham and John Stephenson, *Top Tips on Discovering the Bible with Children*, Bletchley: Scripture Union, 2009.

Two websites developed through the partnership of several Christian agencies provide (1) the KidsGames Bible and sports-related curriculum for outreach related to global sports events such as the Olympic Games and the Soccer World Cup; there are also values-based programmes; (2) general resources for children's ministry developed as a result of KidsGames:

http://www.kidsgames.com

http://www.max7.org

Chapter 8. Church's Word

David Day, *Embodying the Word* (London: SPCK, 2005) is a brilliantly practical book on preaching.

Richard Foster with Kathryn A. Helmers, *Life with God: A Life-Transforming New Approach to Bible Reading* (London: Hodder & Stoughton, 2008) is about reading Scripture in order to live it.

Philip Jenkins, *The New Faces of Christianity: Believing the Bible in the Global South* (Oxford, O.U.P., 2006) is an important and fascinating study of how the church in the global South is engaging with the Bible.

Appendix 2

Statement of Hermeneutical Principles[207]

Scripture Union has adopted the following hermeneutical principles for use by editors, writers and all who handle the Bible on behalf of the movement.

Rather than being seen as options on a menu, these principles are to be taken as a whole and taken together, are to govern our approach every time we come to Scripture. The emphasis placed on each one may vary on different occasions, but all should be informing our thinking, at least implicitly.

We believe that the Bible should be interpreted:

a) **Prayerfully,** in humility and in dependence on the Holy Spirit. We come to Scripture acknowledging that only the Holy Spirit can open our blind eyes and illumine our dark hearts to what God is saying. As God's empowering presence, the Spirit will lead people to engage with the text and to face God's challenge in the here and now. The recognition that the Holy Spirit brings a sense of immediacy will draw us into an understanding, not just of the original meaning of the text, but also of its contemporary prophetic significance.

b) **Corporately rather than simply individualistically.** We are the body of Christ. We stand in a line of historical interpretation that we respect, and from which we learn. As we engage with Scripture together, greater understanding emerges, fellowship is deepened and appropriation encouraged.

c) **As a whole.** We are committed to the whole of Scripture, to allowing Scripture to interpret Scripture, and to promote the understanding of the broad sweep of God's dealings with humanity from creation to **new** creation. In doing this we affirm that the Bible is a metanarrative;

that is, it tells a story which gives meaning to all of life, and by which all of life must be judged. In terms of this metanarrative, we will emphasize interpretation both as propositional and as a response to this metanarrative, and help people to enter imaginatively into the biblical story, seeking always to lead them to live under its authority.

- **Contextually – as it was written.** The Bible contains different literary forms (genres) and the way God **communicates** often differs from one to another. Therefore interpretation includes recognizing and respecting the genre of each passage. The passage is then to be interpreted according to the author's intention and in terms of its historical and canonical context. To the criticism that, however desirable this may be, it is unattainable, we assert that, while exhaustive knowledge of these things may be impossible, adequate knowledge is not.

- **Contextually – as it is encountered.** Our presuppositions, culture, gender, age, and personal history – in short, all that is going on in our lives and communities – always colour our encounter with Scripture. Every encounter is an interpretation. Nevertheless we can know and experience scriptural truth; and while our **communities** exercise a significant influence on our understanding of Scripture, they are not ultimately a binding force. We need constantly to bring our understanding of Scripture back to Scripture. At the same time we need to listen to the interpretation of Scripture of others who belong to different contexts, so that our understanding may be enriched and our blind spots corrected.

- **Contextually – as it is lived out.** Encountering God through his Word will have an impact on our lives, encouraging us in worship, mission, and holiness. As we commit ourselves to obeying God's Word, our experience will help us to understand the Bible better, and deepen our faith in, and our fellowship with, God.

- **Christologically.** Jesus Christ (his birth and life on earth, his death and resurrection, his ascension and second coming) is God's key **Word** in his dealings with human beings; and he, therefore, is the focus of God's revelation in the Bible. Our basic aim states that meeting God through the Bible and prayer will lead to personal faith in Christ. The Holy Spirit leads us into the truth, always testifying to and glorifying Jesus. In the light of these things, in engaging with the Bible, we should consider how a passage ultimately relates to Jesus Christ.

- **Relationally:** a meeting with God. We do not read the Bible simply to collect information about God. Rather, through the stories, promises, commands, warnings and examples, we begin to understand God, meet with him and know him personally. To attempt to interpret Scripture and yet somehow to stop short of enjoying that relationship of love, is to miss the entire purpose for which God, whose nature is love, has revealed himself in the Bible. God is a relational God, his character is to build and sustain relationships. So all our interpretation of Scripture is to be rooted in the two dimensions of our relatedness to God as his children, and of the web of human relationships around us.

Fundamentally, engaging with the Bible is about a relationship with God, and this can only be achieved by dependence on the Holy Spirit.

NOTES

1. These events took place during a Hosanna Ministries 'Faith Comes by Hearing' programme in Bolivia. I am indebted to Morgan Jackson of Hosanna Ministries for this anecdote and the following one about Nurat.
2. In the Old Testament the word translated 'eunuch' means 'an officer of the court' with the secondary meaning of a man who has been castrated (so that the official could move freely among the women of the court). In Acts 8:27 Luke probably intends both meanings in his use of the Greek *eunouchos*. As a castrate, this man would not have been allowed to become a Jewish proselyte (Deut. 23:1) and would have been able to worship only in the outer 'Court of the Gentiles' in the Jerusalem temple.
3. Interview with Dr Jerip Susil, Kuching, Sarawak, September 2008.
4. Interview and written testimony by Revd David Bruce, Executive Director, Board of Mission of the Presbyterian Church in Ireland.
5. Will Hutton, 'The Jubilee line that works', *Observer*, October 3, 1999.
6. Tim Adams, 'A good man in Africa', *The Observer Food Monthly*, November 2005, No. 56.
7. Andrew Rugasira, personal email, 19 November, 2005.
8. Nigel Sylvester, *God's Word in a Young World*, London: Scripture Union, 1984, p. 141.
9. Sylvester, Ibid., pp. 141–142.
10. Will Hutton, 'The Jubilee line that works', *Observer*, October 3, 1999.
11. Paragraph 2, 'The Authority and Power of the Bible' at www.lausanne.org/lausanne-1974/lausanne-covenant.html.
12. Kevin Vanhoozer, *Is There a Meaning in This Text?* Leicester: Apollos / Inter-Varsity Press, 1998, pp. 456–457, 467.
13. Ibid., p. 467.
14. Carlos Mesters, *Defenseless Flower: A New Reading of the Bible*, Maryknoll, New York: Orbis Books, 1989, p. 56.
15. Bob Ekblad, *Reading the Bible with the Damned*, Louisville, Kentucky: Westminster John Knox Press, 2005, pp. 26–27.
16. See, for example, Derek Kidner, who describes the serpent's contradiction in Genesis 3:4 in these terms: 'It is the serpent's word against God's, and the first doctrine to be denied is judgment' (*Genesis*, Tyndale Old Testament Commentaries, Leicester: IVP, 1967, p. 68).
17. Ricoeur, Paul, *The Symbolism of Evil*, Boston: Beacon Press, 1969, p. 250.
18. Bob Ekblad, *Reading the Bible with the Damned*, pp. 28–30.
19. David Smith, *Moving Towards Emmaus: Hope in a Time of Uncertainty*, London: SPCK

2007, pp. 39, 75, my italics.

20. Claudio Ettl, *Bulletin Dei Verbum*, Stuttgart: Catholic Biblical Federation, No. 74/75, 2005, English edition, p. 3.

21. Isaac Phiri and Joe Maxwell, 'Gospel Riches', *Christianity Today*, July 2007. The article is available on http://www.christianitytoday.com/ct/2007/july/12.22.html.

22. Ibid.

23. Christopher Wright, *The Mission of God: Unlocking the Bible's Grand Narrative*, Downers Grove: InterVarsity Press, 2006, pp. 215–216, my italics.

24. Kapolyo, Joe M., *The Human Condition: Christian Perspectives Through African Eyes*, Leicester: Inter-Varsity Press, 2005, p. 126.

25. Ibid., p. 126.

26. Ibid., p. 133.

27. Ibid., pp. 141–142.

28. Ibid., pp. 137–138.

29. David Smith, *Moving Towards Emmaus*, pp. 75–76.

30. Johann Kinghorn, 'On the theology of church and society in the DRC [Dutch Reformed Church]', *Journal of Theology for Southern Africa* 70 (March 1990), pp.21–36. This article can be viewed at http://web.uct.ac.za/depts/ricsa/jtsa/

31. The International Commission of Jurists, Geneva, editors, *The Trial of Beyers Naudé: Christian witness and the rule of law*, 1975, London: Search Press in conjunction with Ravan Press, Johannesburg, 1975, p. 56.

32. Ibid., p. 59.

33. Ibid., pp. 68, 69, 73.

34. Beyers Naudé, C.F. and Dorothee Sölle (1986), *Hope for Faith: A Conversation*, Geneva: WCC Publications / Grand Rapids: Eerdmans, pp. 6–7.

35. Ibid., p. 7.

36. www.polity.org.za/article.php?a_id=57134

37. Gerald O. West and Musa W. Dube, editors, *The Bible in Africa: Transactions, Trajectories and Trends*, Leiden: Brill, 2000, p. 25.

38. Carlos Mesters, 'A "Liberating Reading" of the Bible', originally published in Portuguese in *Medellín*, No.88, Vol. XXII, December 1996, pp. 123–138 and available in English on the website of the Catholic Biblical Federation www.c-b-f.org under 'Biblical Pastoral Ministry'.

39. Ida Glaser, *The Bible and Other Faiths*, Leicester: IVP, 2005, p. 36.

40. Justo L. González, *Santa Biblia: The Bible Through Hispanic Eyes*, Nashville: Abingdon, 1996, p. 23.

41. Ibid., p. 25.

42. Walter Brueggemann, *The Book That Breathes New Life: Scriptural Authority and Biblical Theology*, Minneapolis: Augsburg Fortress, 2005, p. 3.

43. Both the Nicene Creed and the Westminster Confession may be found on www. reformed.org/documents/

44. *Dogmatic Constitution on Divine Revelation*, Chapter 3, Section 11, available on www. vatican.va/archive/hist_councils/ii_vatican_council/index.htm

45. Lausanne Committee for World Evangelization, *The Lausanne Covenant*, 1974, Section 2. The text of the *Covenant* is available at www.lausanne.org/covenant

46. N. T. Wright, *Scripture and the Authority of God*, London: SPCK, 2005, pp. 17, 18.

47. David Smith, *Against the Stream*, Leicester: IVP, 2003, p. 123.

48. Augustine, *Confessions*, Book 8.12.29 available on http://www9.georgetown.edu/faculty/

jod/Englishconfessions.html

49. Augustine, *Homilies on the Gospel of John*, Tractate XLII, available on http://www.ccel. org/ccel/schaff/npnf107.iii.xliii.html

50. N. T. Wright, *Scripture and the Authority of God*, p. 19.

51. Paul Ricoeur has made some of the most important contributions to our understanding of the role of the imagination in engaging the will and changing behaviour. See, for example, 'Listening to the Parables of Jesus' in Charles E. Reagan & David Stewart, Editors, *The Philosophy of Paul Ricoeur, An Anthology of his Work*, Boston, Beacon Press, 1978, pp. 239-245.

52. Walter Brueggemann, *Finally Comes the Poet: Daring Speech for Proclamation*, Minneapolis: Augsburg Fortress, 1989, pp. 1, 2.

53. Ype Schaaf, *L'Histoire et le Rôle de la Bible en Afrique*, Collection 'Défi Africain' and Editions des Groupes Missionnaires, Lavigny, 1994, p. 219 (my translation).

54. Justo González, p. 115.

55. Carlos Mesters, 'A "Liberating Reading" of the Bible', available on the website of the Catholic Biblical Federation, http://www.c-b-f.org

56. See I. Howard Marshall, *Biblical Inspiration*, London: Hodder and Stoughton, 1982, pp. 31–47.

57. Ibid., pp. 44, 46.

58. Eugene H. Peterson, *Eat This Book: a Conversation in the Art of Spiritual Reading*, Grand Rapids: Eerdmans, 2006, pp. 71, 72.

59. Origen, Homily 34.3, Joseph T. Lienhard, trans., *Origen, Homilies on Mark, Fragments on Mark* (1996), p. 38.

60. Brendan W. Devitt, 'What is hermeneutics?' *Lion and Lamb* 19, 1998/99, p. 5. Available online at http://www.contemporarychristianity.net/lionandlamb/lion&lamb_back. htm#16

61. Gerald Bray, *Biblical Interpretation Past and Present*, Downers Grove: InterVarsity Press, 1996, p. 82.

62. Kevin J. Vanhoozer, *Is There a Meaning in This Text?* Leicester: Apollos / Inter-Varsity Press, 1998, p. 115.

63. Quoted in Robert M. Grant with David Tracy, *A Short History of the Interpretation of the Bible*, London: SCM, 1984, p. 94.

64. Quoted in Vanhoozer, *Is There a Meaning in This Text?* p. 118.

65. Vanhoozer, *Is There a Meaning in This Text?* p. 119.

66. Ibid., p. 135.

67. Melba Maggay, unpublished transcript of a lecture, used by permission.

68. Vanhoozer, p. 205.

69. Melba Maggay.

70. Jacob A. Loewen, *The Bible in Cross-Cultural Perspective*, Pasadena: William Carey Library, 2000, pp. 59–61.

71. N. T. Wright, *Scripture and the Authority of God*, London: SPCK, 2005, p. 11.

72. Eugene H. Peterson, *Eat This Book*, Grand Rapids: Eerdmans, 2006, p. 125.

73. Scripture Union International Council, 'Statement of Hermeneutical Principles', 2001. The full document can be found in Appendix 2.

74. Enzo Bianchi, *Praying the Word: An Introduction to Lectio Divina*, Kalamazoo: Cistercian Publications, 1998, p. 42.

75. Lesley Smith, *Medieval Exegesis in Translation: Commentaries on the book of Ruth*, Kalamazoo: Medieval Institute Publications, 1996, p. 65.

76. John Wesley, *Explanatory Notes on the Bible*, published between 1754 and 1765, available online on websites such as www.biblestudytools.com/commentaries/

77. Richard Bauckham, *Is The Bible Male? The Book of Ruth and Biblical Narrative*, Cambridge: Grove, 1996, p. 10.

78. Lausanne Committee for World Evangelisation, *The Lausanne Covenant*, 1974, paragraph 9, www.lausanne.org.

79. Samuel Escobar, *La Fe Evangélica y las Teologías de la Liberación*, El Paso: Casa Bautista de Publicaciones, 1987, pp. 171–172, my translation.

80. Bauckham, *Is The Bible Male?* p. 3.

81. Eugene Peterson, *Working the Angles: The Shape of Pastoral Integrity*, Grand Rapids: Eerdmans, 1987, p. 86.

82. N. T. Wright, *Scripture and the Authority of God*, London: SPCK, 2005, p. 97.

83. A helpful survey of different expressions of the idea of the Bible as a drama can be found in J. Richard Middleton and Brian J. Walsh, *Truth is Stranger Than It Used To Be: Biblical Faith in a Postmodern Age*, London: SPCK, 1995, pp. 181–183.

84. Christopher J. H. Wright, 'Interpreting the Bible Among the World's Religions', *Themelios* Vol 25:3, available on http://www.thegospelcoalition.org/publications

85. N. T. Wright , *Scripture and the Authority of God*, pp. 98–99.

86. Christopher J. H. Wright, *The Mission of God*, pp. 48–49.

87. Eugene H. Peterson, *Eat This Book: A Conversation in the Art of Spiritual Reading*, Grand Rapids: Eerdmans, 2006, pp. 70, 71.

88. Ibid., p. 71.

89. Christopher J. H. Wright, *The Mission of God*, p. 53.

90. Vanhoozer, p. 465.

91. Vanhoozer, p. 467.

92. Richard Holloway, 'The End that never came', *The Scotsman*, 3 January 2000.

93. Eugene Peterson, *Reversed Thunder: The Revelation of John and the Praying Imagination*, New York: Harper & Row, 1988, pp. xi, xii.

94. Tom Wright, *Paul for Everyone: Romans, Part 1*, London: SPCK, 2004, p. 46.

95. Peter Craigie, *The Problem of War in the Old Testament*, Grand Rapids: Eerdmans, 1978.

96. Ibid., p. 10.

97. Ibid., p. 38.

98. Ibid., p. 70.

99. In his book *Violence* (New York: Seabury, 1969, pp.84–93), Jacques Ellul, the French Christian social critic and theologian, makes an eloquent case for the inevitability of violence in the founding and maintenance of any state.

100. Carl von Clausewitz's definition of war quoted in Craigie, p. 46.

101. Craigie, pp. 40, 43.

102. Ibid., p. 74.

103. René Padilla, 'With love from Argentina', *Third Way*, October 1982, pp. 28, 29.

104. Craigie, pp. 76–81.

105. On this issue, Craigie (p.27) quotes Michael Walzer, 'Exodus 32 and the Theory of Holy War: The History of a Citation', *Harvard Theological Review*, 61 (1968), 3–14.

106. The website http://www.aolnews.com/story/pentagon-briefings-carried-bible-verses/487977 reveals how cynically Scripture can be used for political ends.

107. Scripture Union International, 'Statement of Hermeneutical Principles'. See Appendix 2, p. 145.

108. Richard Bauckham, *Gospel Women: Studies of the Named Women in the Gospels*,

Edinburgh: Eerdmans and T. & T. Clark, 2002, pp. xv, xvi.

109. Scripture Union, 'Statement of Hermeneutical Principles'.

110. Richard Bauckham makes a strong historical and linguistic case for Junia being the same woman as Joanna, the wife of Herod's steward Chuza, mentioned in Luke 8:2 among the women who financed Jesus' ministry and in Luke 24:10 as being among the first witnesses of the resurrection (*Gospel Women*, pp. 109–202).

111. Helmut Thielicke (trans. John W. Doberstein), *The Ethics of Sex*, New York: Harper & Row, 1964, p. 8.

112. Bob Ekblad, personal prayer letter, July 2009. See also www.sorat.ukzn.ac.za/ujamaa/default.htm

113. David Smith, *Moving Towards Emmaus, Hope in a Time of Uncertainty*, London: SPCK, 2007, p. 47.

114. Marva J. Dawn, *Sexual Character: Beyond Technique to Intimacy*, Grand Rapids: Eerdmans 1993, p. 91.

115. Ted Grimsrud and Mark Thiessen Nation, *Reasoning Together: A Conversation on Homosexuality*, Scottdale, Pa.: Herald Press, 2008, p. 226.

116. Dawn, p. 94.

117. Tom Wright, *Paul for Everyone: Romans, Part 1*, London: SPCK, 2004, pp. 22–24.

118. Richard B. Hays, 'Relations Natural and Unnatural: A Response to John Boswell's Exegesis of Romans 1', *The Journal of Religious Ethics* 4, 1 (Spring 1986), p. 199.

119. Pew Foundation, *World Publics Welcome Global Trade – But Not Immigration*, Global Attitudes Report, 2007, available on http://pewglobal.org/reports

120. Dawn, p. 107.

121. Kathleen Norris writes movingly of her friendship with a monk: 'This was celibacy at its best, a man's sexual energies so devoted to the care of others that a few words could lift me out of despair, give me the strength to reclaim my life. Abundance indeed.' (*The Cloister Walk*, Oxford, Lion, 2000, p.139). This is surely a description of the life of Jesus!

122. Sultan Muhammed Paul, *Why I Became a Christian*, Chapter 9, 'Quest for Salvation', The Good Way Publishing, 2010, available on http://www.the-good-way.com

123. Peter Riddell, 'Themes and Resources in Christian–Muslim Relations', *Anvil*, Vol. 23, No. 2, 2006. The article is available on http://www.anviljournal.co.uk/Editorials/23_2.htm

124. C. E. Padwick, *Temple Gairdner of Cairo*, London: SPCK, 1929, pp. 179–180.

125. Prayer letter from Muslim Peoples International mission partners, March 2006.

126. Prayer letter from Muslim Peoples International mission partners, August 2006.

127. Prayer letter from Muslim Peoples International mission partners, November 2006.

128. Ida Glaser, *The Bible and Other Faiths: What Does the Lord Require of Us?* Leicester: Inter-Varsity Press, 2005.

129. Abdullah Yusuf Ali, translator, *The Holy Qur'an: Text, Translation and Commentary*, Brentwood, Maryland: Amana Corporation, 1989, pp. 14, 15.

130. Homepage of www.jannah.org.

131. John Burton, *The Collection of the Qur'an*, Cambridge: C.U.P., 1977, p. 11.

132. See, for example, www.understandingislam.com

133. See, for example, www.al-islam.org/quran/

134. Abdullah Yusuf Ali, translator, *The Holy Qur'an: Text, Translation and Commentary*, pp. 747, 748.

135. Ida Glaser, 'Reading the Bible in the Context of Islam', *UBS Journal*, Pune, India: Union Biblical Seminary, Vol. 3 No. 1, 2005, pp. 82–101.

136. Seyed Hossein Nasr, 'Responses to Hans Küng's paper on Christian–Muslim Dialogue',

The Muslim World, Vol. 77, Issue 2, 1987, p. 98.

137. Kenneth Cragg, *The Call of the Minaret*, London: Collins, 1986, pp. 247, 248.

138. Fazlur Rahman, *Islam*, London: University of Chicago Press, 1979, p. 31.

139. Ibn Khaldun, *The Muqaddimah*, p. 74, quoted in Steven Masood, *The Bible and the Qur'an*, p. 7.

140. Steven Masood, *The Bible and the Qur'an*, Carlisle, OM Publishing, 2001, pp. 7–9.

141. Ida Glaser, 'Reading the Bible in the Context of Islam', *UBS Journal,* Pune, India: Union Biblical Seminary, Vol. 3 No. 1, 2005, pp. 82–101.

142. Abdullah Yusuf Ali, translator, *The Holy Qur'an: Text, Translation and Commentary*, pp. 1164–1167.

143. Salman Ghaffari, Iranian ambassador to the Vatican, quoted in Jean-Marie Gaudeul, *Called from Islam to Christ: Why Muslims Become Christians*, Monarch Books, 1999, p. 31.

144. Sally Sutcliffe (Editor), *Good News for Asians in Britain*, Church Army and the Grove Evangelism Series, No. 43, 1998, p. 18.

145. Abdullah Yusuf Ali, translator, *The Holy Qur'an: Text, Translation and Commentary*, p. 1714.

146. Ibid., pp. 239, 240.

147. Kenneth Cragg, p. 279.

148. Abdullah Yusuf Ali, translator, *The Holy Qur'an: Text, Translation and Commentary*, Surah 4, 157, 158, pp. 235, 236.

149. Ibid., p. 236, footnote 663.

150. Kenneth Cragg, p. 265.

151. Ibid., p. 268.

152. Ibid., p. 325.

153. I cited this story, which I heard on the radio, in the editorial of Scripture Union International's *Catalyst*, Issue 2, August 2007, p. 1, available on http://www.su-international.org/

154. Ivy Beckwith, *Postmodern Children's Ministry: Ministry to Children in the 21st Century*, Grand Rapids Zondervan, 2004, p. 126.

155. Ibid., p. 131.

156. *Catalyst*, Issue 2, August 2007, p. 7.

157. Wendy Strachan, 'Opening up the Bible with Children', *Catalyst*, Issue 2, August 2007, p. 2.

158. Naomi Swindon, *Six Windows*, unpublished resource.

159. Beckwith, p. 136.

160. More information about Godly Play can be found on a range of websites. The main site is www.godlyplay.org

161. Reported in 2005 by Andrew Ramsbottom, Scripture Union New Zealand.

162. Leanne Palmer, Sydney, Australia, personal communication.

163. Beckwith, p. 130.

164. Ibid., p. 130.

165. Glenn M. Cupit, 'Towards a biblical hermeneutic for children and those like them', available under the list of publications on http://www.unisanet.unisa.edu.au/staff/Homepage.asp?Name=glenn.cupit

166. Ibid., p. 3.

167. Ibid., p. 5.

168. Ibid., p. 7.

169. Ibid., p. 8.

170. Terry Clutterham, *The Adventure Begins: a Practical Guide to Exploring the Bible with Under-12s*, London: Scripture Union 1996, pp. 35, 36.

171. Scripture Union International, *Catalyst*, Issue 1, February 2007, p. 10, available on http://www.su-international.org/

172. Clayton Fergie has developed this idea into a 'Timelining Scripture' workshop. The resource is available on www.scripture-engagement.org/ if you subscribe to the 'Community' feature.

173. Carlos Mesters, *Defenseless Flower*, 1989, p. 74.

174. N. T. Wright, *Scripture and the Authority of God*, p. 29.

175. Ibid., pp. 35, 36.

176. 'It used to be said that the New Testament writers "didn't think they were writing 'scripture'". That is hard to sustain historically today ... At precisely those points of urgent need (when, for instance, writing Galatians or 2 Corinthians) Paul is most conscious that he is writing as one authorized, by the apostolic call he had received from Jesus Christ, and in the power of the Spirit, to bring life and order to the church by his words', N. T. Wright, *Scripture and the Authority of God*, p. 37.

177. F. F. Bruce, *The Books and the Parchments*, London: Pickering and Inglis, 1971, pp. 11, 12; Tom Wright, *Paul for Everyone: The Pastoral Letters*, SPCK, 2003, pp. 131, 132.

178. Shane Hipps, *The Hidden Power of Electronic Culture*, Grand Rapids: Zondervan, 2005, p. 51.

179. Ibid., pp. 53, 54.

180. Tim Conder and Daniel Rhodes, *Free for All: Rediscovering the Bible in Community*, Grand Rapids: Baker Books, 2009, p. 13.

181. Eugene H. Peterson, *Eat This Book*, pp. 81, 82.

182. Ibid., p. 90, my italics.

183. Dietrich Bonhöffer, *Life Together*, London: SCM, 1954, p. 28.

184. Stephen E. Fowl and L. Gregory Jones, *Reading in Communion: Scripture and Ethics in Christian Life*, London: SPCK, 1991, p. 145.

185. Henri Bacher, 'The Bible in the Future', paper in French and English, available on http://www.scripture-engagement.org/

186. *Dei Verbum*, available on www.vatican.va/archive/hist_councils/ii_vatican_council/documents/vat-ii_const_19651118_dei-verbum_en.html

187. N. T. Wright, *Scripture and the Authority of God*, p. 97.

188. Richard Bauckham, *The Gospels as Eyewitness Testimony*, Cambridge: Grove, 2008.

189. Eugene H. Peterson, *Working the Angles: The Shape of Pastoral Integrity*, Grand Rapids: Eerdmans, 1987, p. 86.

190. Unlock's approaches and resources can be seen on their website www.unlock-urban.org.uk/

191. United Bible Societies, *Manual de Lectio Divina para Jóvenes Misioneros*, Colombia: 2006, p. 3, my translation.

192. http://e100nz.org.nz/

193. Henri Bacher, 'The Bible in the Future'.

194. Review of a performance of Mark's Gospel in Chicago in 2009, http://chicago.broadwayworld.com/article/MARKS_GOSPEL_Makes_Chicago_Premiere_At_Mercury_Theater_423517_20090330

195. From a sermon by Dr Stephen Cherry available on www.durhamcathedral.co.uk/schedule/sermons/123. Professor Grace Davie's paper is 'Seeing Salvation: The use

of data as text in the sociology of religion', in Avis, P. (ed), *Public Faith? The State of Religious Belief and Practice in Britain*, London: SPCK, 2003, pp. 28–44.

196. Tom Wright, *Paul for Everyone, Romans, Part 2*, London: SPCK, 2004, p. 111.

197. Eugene H. Peterson, *Reversed Thunder: The Revelation of John and the Praying Imagination*, New York: Harper & Row, 1988, p. 23.

198. N. T. Wright, *Scripture and the Authority of God*, p. 89.

199. Ibid., p. 90.

200. Carlos Mesters, *Defenceless Flower*, pp. 117, 118.

201. Tom Wright, *Matthew for Everyone, Part 2*, London: SPCK, 2002, pp. 99, 100.

202. Personal prayer letter.

203. David Zac Niringiye, 'Integral Mission' in SU International *Catalyst* No 1, 2006.

204. The seven key factors identified by the Forum of Bible Agencies International as being of the highest priority are listed in Daryl Balia and Kirsteen Kim (eds.), *Edinburgh 2010, Volume II, Witnessing to Christ Today*, Oxford: Regnum, 2010, p. 266. The book is available on www.edinburgh2010.org/

205. Tom Wright, *Matthew for Everyone*, p. 80.

206. J. Richard Middleton and Brian J. Walsh, *Truth Is Stranger Than It Used To Be*, p. 184.

207. The first draft of these Principles was drawn up by Neil Dougall, Andrew Clark, John Grayston and David Bruce. The draft was circulated to Scripture Union movements around the world for comment and the final version was agreed at a consultation in 2001. An interesting reflection on these principles from an African perspective can be found in Andrew Olu Igenoza, 'Contextual balancing of Scripture with Scripture: Scripture Union in Nigeria and Ghana', in Gerald O. West and Musa W. Dube, *The Bible in Africa: Transactions, Trajectories and Trends*, Leiden: Brill, 2000, pp. 292–310.